I excel

WIRED FOR SUCCESS

Personal Excellence Blueprint

DAVID NAIR

notionpress
.com

INDIA · SINGAPORE · MALAYSIA

Notion Press

No. 8, 3rd Cross Street,
CIT Colony, Mylapore,
Chennai, Tamil Nadu – 600 004

First Published by Notion Press 2020
Copyright © David Nair 2020
All Rights Reserved.

ISBN 978-1-63633-670-1

This book has been published with all efforts taken to make the material error-free after the consent of the author. However, the author and the publisher do not assume and hereby disclaim any liability to any party for any loss, damage, or disruption caused by errors or omissions, whether such errors or omissions result from negligence, accident, or any other cause.

While every effort has been made to avoid any mistake or omission, this publication is being sold on the condition and understanding that neither the author nor the publishers or printers would be liable in any manner to any person by reason of any mistake or omission in this publication or for any action taken or omitted to be taken or advice rendered or accepted on the basis of this work. For any defect in printing or binding the publishers will be liable only to replace the defective copy by another copy of this work then available.

Contents

Acknowledgements

A personal Thank You to all those who played an important part in my life. I truly would not be where I am today if it was not for my parents, family, relatives, friends, fourteen mentors and the thousands of people who have been there to love, guide, teach, support, motivate, inspire and provide clarity to steer me through this journey of life.

This book is also dedicated to the thousands of participants who have attended my programs over the last two and half decades. Sincere thank you to those who have been accepting the principles and patterns for change and believing in the transformation stories to step up in their own life and live a life they only dreamed of in the past.

A special thank you to my mentors and gurus who like a sculptor would wheel a lump of clay, and artfully sculpt out a magnificent vase. They could see the quality of the clay when I had little belief in myself, they would drip droplets of water to moisten the clay and put pressure with their thumbs kneading the clay to turn it into the perfect vase. A sincere and heartfelt thank you to them for being extremely patient. When you hear my story later, you will understand where I was and how I have worked to reach where I am today.

The Empowered You

Your passport to a better Tomorrow

- davidnair

Why I Wrote This Book

The journey from a practicing CPA, a VP of the third largest Oil & Gas Company, to being an author, key-note International Speaker, Personal Excellence Peak Performance Coach/Mentor and Philanthropist is nothing short of interesting, especially when we are working with the development of people.

I have had the privilege of working with a wide spectrum of people ranging from business entrepreneurs through to corporate professions, from varying industries and career levels. The Coaching, Mentoring & Training conducted, ranged from new University/College recruits through to middle management, senior management, country heads and CEO's of organizations. The following are what triggered me to write this book.

A Balanced Holistic Life

Over the last 20 years, I have managed to impact thousands of supervisors, managers, VP's, and a handful of CEOs and 200,000+ of their subordinates, associates and friends, entrepreneurs and business proprietors with my coaching and training. One primary learning that I received out of working in the trenches was that many people are exceptional good in their own domain of expertise, Information Technology, Banking, Accounting, Sales, Hospitality, Service driven etc. But when it comes to living a holistic balanced life, questions are raised. I ask: Why is a balanced life not achievable? What is stopping that achievement? What is the problem that a holistic life seems to be impossible to achieve? How do we achieve it? Where do I need to go to be aware of it? Etc, etc, etc. Fret not, for as you journey through this book a few of these questions will be answered. Other revelations will be unfolded at our workshops.

What I am sharing and expressing in this book is not theory, or one person's experience, they are real-life patterns, tools and exercises used daily by many within my tribe and have found a balanced holistic Life.

They are testimony of how these practices have altered their states and life. This *Modus Operand for Life Excellence is* the Blueprint for excellence that I refer to as *I-eXceL – Wired For Success.* The live heartbeat for the blueprint to excellence will be found at the detailed three-day residential workshop, held at a location near you. Do lock up with us through our social media sites, to know the details of the events. The links to the sites will be found in the last chapter of this book.

The 3 E's to Our Education

Our main frame of knowledge within us, acquired over the years, comes from numerous sources, which could be grouped into three primary categories - Education, Experience and Exposure, which we at IXL Inc, (the company I set up for such development work) commonly refer to as the 3E's of life education. Our whole of life education could be summed up as originating from these three sources.

To ensure you acquire the most out of this book, we have created a segment called *"My 10 Minutes"*. As you read through this book, please do the exercises, and see how you Build yourself. The mastery of these specific skillset will provide the excellence blueprint that most of us strife for and many do not achieve it even when they retire. This is done for you to continuously, reflect upon, introspect, and scale up your daily self-practices. This consistent practice over time will shift you towards being that person you genuinely want to be.

Please ensure you do every exercise no matter how simple some of them might be. You will just need to do it to sequentially to go through the process to Build You.

I would also recommend that you get a notebook – a journal where you can jot down points, as you wade through the various sections. Wherever you find some sections, you are very good at or mastered, highlight those as empowering practices that you have in you, anchor on these practices and whenever you are on a downer, reach out of that segment and image that segment several times in your mind. You will be surprised how uplifting and empowering this can be for you, especially when you feel all else is not going your way.

On the other hand, whenever you find some part where it niggles you to do something about it, or you are frustrated about that segment of life or thing that you constantly angry about in your life: what would you want to do about it? You want to change that behavior but have never been able to find the time resource or inclination to do so. In these instances, jot down the points. Do a self-evaluation. What are the circumstances that has caused you to do certain things, say certain things, behavior in a certain manner, the endless disempowering feelings, actions, thoughts resulting in the outcomes that you never envisioned to be in? How would you like to change? What if you were able to find the solution and change? What would your life be like? Image that into you, and for now focus on that area that you want to transform. Write it down.

"My 10 Minute" Reflection on 3 E's

Reverting to the above discussion of the 3 E's. Stop for a moment and reflect on it, spend some time by yourself and do what I commonly refer to as a dip stick check. For each of the three categories, **Education, Exposure and Experience**, measure on a scale of 1 to 10, from where did you acquire your current knowledge? Why is this important, for any transformation to take place we need to know our current position? Our start position and how to kick start it for a sprint, a marathon. Its identical to the starting block that athletes use for their races. Their kick start for their 100-meter sprint, and all other races like the 200-meter 1000 meter and subsequent races. Our race of life is the same.

As an example, we would wade through the following questions. How much of your current knowledge comes from Mainstream education? Primary school, secondary school, tertiary school, college, or university. How much of the current knowledge comes from experience, particularly experience of others, this opens the domain of seeking a mentor, coach for yourself or being one to others – role model. How much of it comes from exposure. The interaction with others from the same community, work area, interacting within one culture and or being cross culture sensitized. Please understand this is a self-assessment exercise, so do be realistic in your own assessment. Be hard on yourself by being brutally honest. You are not competing or outsmarting anyone else. You just want to know your current position. Where are you in life now. Start questioning yourself why you have not pursued knowledge from the other areas. Would it have helped you acquire a better understand of life balance, if so, why not commence pursuing that?

This is opening a pandora's box on self-introspection. Hence in most cases, decision is being made on limited information, due to being shielded from a lack in the 3E's. It is similar to when someone goes to a buffet luncheon to select a dish from the array of dishes served on the buffet table. Similarly, individuals lack the appreciation of focusing on career or business, there is an untapped part to a Life out there. A segment of life that needs to be plough, seeded, nurtured, fertilized for the harvest of life to yield the return that they truly deserve. Many are unaware of what this really is....

The ROI of Your Life

For some of us who are data driven, analytical and who need a reason to move up, let me slice this cake in such a way that you could appreciate this idea better. Many are unaware of the quadrants that make up their life. Many are unaware of the rate of return that they will need to work at to acquire maximum return on their investment - THEMSELF. Many do not see or have spent time reflecting on their rate of return of the investment their parents put on them. Their parents paid for their education in many cases went through huge hardship to ensure they gave their best for their kids. What is their return on investment? A monthly salary pay check, or is it more. If it was a monthly salary pay check, then they are still mentally tuned in to earning as what the banks would put it, a simple interest rate. Why have they not progressed to look at earning a compound interest on their initial investment, where the returns are many folds higher?

Hence this triggered me to look at what is compound interest for people development. Simply put, it's everything inclusive of mainstream education... For ease I have reverted to a basic mathematical formula that goes as follows:

$$ROI = IQ + EQ + FQ + SQ + SQ$$

Many would cry out, "What does this all mean?" to me and my life. Let me walk you through the base understand of what each of these components mean and later work on its transformation based on your self-assessment

ROI – Rate of Investment in you, your mainstream education that you have gone through to get you to where you are today, coupled with your continuous education that you will be going through to the day you die.

IQ – Intelligence Quotient: Your mainstream education on your domain expertise, to now and your continuous education that you are putting into yourself to be at the cutting edge of that industry that you are working in

EQ – Emotional Quotient: Where are you on your emotional understanding of Self, and the people around you. To put it bluntly, your Interpersonal Skills and your Intrapersonal Skills. How good are you in interacting with people and how good are you in understanding, controlling and centering yourself?

FQ – Financial Quotient: Your financial understand of your financial wealth acquisition, trying to maximize on inflows in the form of income and reduce outflows in the form of expenditure. This is not just to live a hand to mouth existence, the appreciation and understand of leaving behind a nest egg. How much and in what areas.

SQ – Social Quotient: This is basically the circle of people around you who range from family, friends, acquaintance, work colleagues through to the outer circle of strangers and in constantly build that network. How well is this established within your circle of influence?

SQ – Spiritual Quotient: This is basically your alignment with the universe in ensuring your core values are in sync. Understanding your values, people around you and the community, and the people you interact with most. Are they in Sync with your ideals, with your belief, with your philosophy to life?

"My 10 Minute" on My ROI

Due to time and space constraint in this book I would sincerely urge you to lock into our workshops for a more detailed appreciation of the above equation ROI = IQ+EQ+FQ+SQ+SQ. For now, I would sincerely urge you to do the exercise of ranking yourself on a scale of 1 to 10 for each of the elements from IQ through to SQ to see where your ROI would stand. Sum up the scores you have put for each of the elements and see where you stand out of 50.

Keep that score as Benchmark for you to look at how you will progress hereafter. As a Self-measure, do this exercise every quarter and see the progress forward.

Many of us do not realize the potential that resides within us. If we only recognize the power within those potentials and things that our bodies and minds do, we will not hesitate in working towards unleashing that inner power.

The Mind/Body Power Within Us

Did you know -

Our heart beats 100,000 times a day without conscious influence.

Our heart pumps 6000 quarts of blood, through our network of blood vessels.

Our network of blood vessel when put end to end will stretch to over 60000 miles.

Our eyes can make over 10 million color distinctions.

Our combined muscle power when pulled in one direction has 25 tons of pulling power.

All of this and a lot more is run by a 3 - pound matter we call our brain.

Can you fathom, how vast the storage capacity of this computer, within you is? When we add to this the operations of the conscious and sub conscious minds, it is one of the most powerful power houses available on this planet. Very few of us have ever stopped still to do a barometer check on our self.

We as human beings do not realize how magnificent, this temple of ours is and how should we treat it every moment of the day. How we should care for it daily – not just by brushing our teeth and having a bath, and whitewashing of our exterior self with cleanser, toner, moisture, make up and deodorant. Instead what do we do, to ourselves regularly to be in tune, I mean really in tune with ourselves, such that we are at the cutting edge of ourselves for maximum peak performance every moment of our life. Many do not really know or understand what is the real make up of our mind, body, and spirit. If we knew, we could twig and learn how to better stretch its performance, and better understand it and nurture it for our betterment.

In summary, I have identified only a few areas why and how we need to work on ourselves to be that person at the cutting edge in performance.

Our workshop *I-eXceL - Wired For Success* conducted in a city near you, will walk you through these elements in greater detail and many other patterns for change described in this book. Do visit our website, landing pages, and attend our one-day free preview for more information on this subject. You will receive a better understanding of what some of the patterns for change are, and how it can help you recognize the magnificence of your body, mind, and spirit (BMS). We will help guide you, how best to care and nurture your BMS for best outcome. Our focus on specific rituals/pattern shift, when to best do it for the most benefit for the BMS, hence unfolding your true potential.

How to Use This Book Effectively

You would have by now guessed this book is a companion to you for the next 90 day. Read it as a workbook that you are going to put your heart and soul doing the *"My 10 Minute"* exercises and practice those exercises regularly for SELF MASTERY.

Friends as you journey through this book you will note we have addressed further change patterns, rituals, list of empowering and disempowering situations that you could work towards for a more comfortable, pleasing, productive and significant life. All it takes is small 10-minute practices by working through *"My 10 Minutes"* exercises. This is scattered through this book at salient points for you to work through and get a better understand of the concept such that you could master the practice and see a better you. The ultimate intent is to learn how to use this hidden power of BMS properly and unleash the magic within each of you, such that you could reflect on your life to see the journey and be proud of the trail blazer of a life you have left behind.

A legacy "Your life of Significance".

Take my Hand
Walk by my side
Let Me help you Step Up
- davidnair

Enjoy This Journey with Us

For any Transformation or Breakthrough to happen, YOU must Change.

For Change to happen YOU need to raise your standards.... It starts with YOU turning **your Should 's to Must's**

How many times have you told yourself what you should do...?

I should lose weight.

I should be more confident.

I should earn more money.

I should have a better relationship.

I should, I should, I should....

People have an endless list of things they believe they should do or follow through. These carry the same weight as a New Year's Resolution. You set your resolutions prior to midnight on the 31st of December. By 3 am the tsunami has come and washed away that wish...

My commitment to each of you that bought this book. Read through the book, making sure you do every exercise that is found in the relevant sections of the book. Practice for 90 Days, the change patterns, discussed in the book. At the end of the 90 days check the New YOU. And see where you are....

Your Friend, Guide, Coach, Mentor and Role Model

- davidnair

Foreword

This book is an introduction to many life changing principles. Some of those principles will be shared here whilst others will be capsuled in the forthcoming book *"Your Why! – The Driver"* Tagline - *"Destiny – Choice or Chance."* There is a great deal of information in this book, some of these ideas will leap at you, others will take some time to unfold. Walk through the book and take whatever you are ready to digest and master that skill. You do not have to absorb all these ideas at once and apply them in your life immediately. There is always a gestation period, for some of these ideas to cement into a person and subsequently be part of that person's life. If you could get one good idea from this book and improve your quality of life, then I feel my writing this book was well worth it.

There will be many concepts, ideas, and terms that I have used, please do not get overanxious or perplexed about it. This is done solely to show you the vastness of what is out there and there are no limitations on the information and ideas that you can acquire. I would put a caveat, if reference is made to a name or a concept and you are not in agreement with it or concur with the idea or philosophy, then replace the word with your own word, or leave that idea and philosophy and move on. This approach was taken solely to initiate/trigger a thinking process in you such that it creates the awareness of the vastness of what is there in the universe for us to soak in, especially in this platform of Self Excellence.

Foreword

Dear David

I consider it as a Great Honor for being able to write about you & your latest Avatar as an Author ✍

To write about you it will take pages & ages... However I shall try to encapsulate whatever I feel about YOU & YOUR contributions as crisply as possible...

As a Life Coach, You have been my first GURU & you are always special!

I still can remember your 1st Curtain Raiser session about Life, where you explained several things which hit me like a ton of Bricks.

Some of them are The Holes in the Bucket , The Balancing Wheel of Life, Under The Carpet syndrome, Konjam adjust Pannunga, & many such simple, yet powerful concepts that really shook me for good & has had a very deep impact in my life ever since!

Every session of yours has been powerful & transforming

Looking back at the years, There have been several instances, where I have not only approached life through your perspective, but also have had your Vocabulary & your mannerisms too...

You have also introduced us to So many wonderful personalities, their speeches, their thoughts, their books and many of which are ingrained & etched in our brains so deeply that they are like ready reckoners which helps us to deal with any situation!

Like what the Tamil Poet Auvvai would say "What is learnt is just a handful of sand, what is to be learnt is as huge as this universe". In that sense how much ever we learn, never seems to be enough... I'm eager to learn from your New Book, And continue to learn and improve myself more...

The topics that you have chosen are the most needed ones for anyone & everyone... To get success, one has to have a clear understanding of the self & the world which is like a maze, with the right framework & taking ownership now, with absolute clarity & awareness, and definitely give our best. For Excellence, There is absolutely no one to compete with, but the self! And like what is said in the Gita... We have the right to perform the action & not the result... if performed best, the best results are waiting to unfold... And for all of this we can only be Grateful to the whole universe and everyone in it for helping us realize these, this moment!

Ever Grateful to you David for being that Guiding Star, The beacon tower, the powerful inspiration to take life full on and live a purposeful life with SMART Goals & Never ending Ambitions & also the Zeal to achieve & live a Zestful & also a Peaceful Life

Filled with Gratitude David

Sincerely yours

Ranganathan T S

Media Anchor, Business Entrepreneur,
Musician, Producer, Director

Introduction/About the Author

I Am a Student of Life

I was only 16 years old when I was kicked out of my home in Malaysia. My parents sent me to Australia for my studies. At the airport, my dad handed over a three-inch-thick book and said read this book. I looked at my Dad in bewilderment, I was gifted a three-inch-thick biography of a shipping magnet. That was the start of my journey in being a student of life. It took me 6 months to finish that book – One key sentence I got from that book – the shipping magnet was asked this question, *"If you had to start your life all over again, what would you do differently?* His response was, *"I would hang around tables where success people met."* He was asked, *"Why?"* His response was, *"At those tables where successful people met, whatever falls off from the table, would be pure gold."*

Initially this did not make sense, but over time I found the profound wisdom from this statement. The power in associating with peer and above, what they discussed amongst themselves is upward, empowering ideas, when put into action the outcome will undoubtedly yield great results.

The start of my journey of converting from a shy mamma's boy to being this strategist, Certified Practicing Accountant, (CPA), a Coach & Mentor, Keynote International Speaker and an Author, with a definite major purpose *"to create a Mind-set, Heart-set and Soul-set shift in 1 million minds, and their next generation, to stretch that little more in each of them, thereby contributing towards a better world for all of us and generations to come. "*

Picture the image of a young shy, frightened kid, in a foreign land, amongst a completely different type of youth, who were more outward, boisterous, go getters. To top it off, being put into a boarding college for upward mobile kids who were on track to complete their matriculation. I had no exposure to living away from home, especially in a foreign land, with a culture of total foreign ideology, way of life, custom etc.

I was extremely shy and backward I was fearful of interacting with people – basically felt inadequate to talk, I would feel this pain in the pits of my stomach. Even whilst at home, in Malaysia, I would hide behind my mother's petticoat to greet friends and relatives that visited our home. That's how shy I was.

The Brothers (teachers) at the college, would constantly encourage me to go talk with the other students. They introduced me to a few of the parents of the students who took me out for the weekends when they came to collect their own kids. A friendship blossomed between one of the kid's fathers and I, who I commonly refer to as Uncle John. I used to frequent their home quite a lot as I got to know Smithy, their son. As time went on, I would spend most weekends at their home. We used to have dinner at the dining table, where Uncle John would talk about his business, ask how others were and what's been happening etc. This was a huge revelation for me, yes, our parents would talk to us but not in the transparent, open and carefree manner that Uncle John interacted with us - kids. I quickly pick up he was a businessperson and was constantly talking about making business deals, banking, letters of credit etc.

More of the journey, challenges encountered and how to get over them is detailed as you weave through the book.

Today after having had the opportunity of working over three decades, with over 250000 people, I think of myself as a stepping stone, guiding individuals on their pathway to self-discovery and working at their best in manifesting their Dreams and goals. I create a space where people can learn, how they can liberate their potential they have within themselves, to excel in their field of passion. As a coach, I work in nurturing them, building the belief they have within themselves. I am a person who empowers people. I help them remove their limiting beliefs based on the education, environment, or experience (the 3 E's). I help them take control of their life's. I guide them in discovering their potential, wisdom, and strength. I guide, and say to them, its ok to fail, and ok to bounce back in life. The measure to see how sustainable they are is simple, the speed in which the bounce back after a fall.

I have been criticized by some in my use of simple techniques and patterns for change... how could such simplistic approach creating transformation within people. Interesting enough the KISS (Keep IT Simple Stupid) works all the time. We create breakthroughs in people by focusing on small things which generates big gains, from an inside out transformation.

The power within is limitless......

The more we learn to connect with that power...

The more we become free in the four quadrants of our life

- davidnair

Having a Purpose in Life

My DEFINITE MAJOR PURPOSE (DMP) is *"to create a Mind-set, Heart-set, Health-set and Soul set, shift in 1 million minds, and their next generation, to stretch that little more in each of them, thereby contributing towards a better world for all of us and generations to come "*

Confidence & Dependence Concern:

I was born in Malaysia and was sent to residency school in Australia at an early age of 15 years to finish my secondary schooling. The primary reason as I put it "being kicked out of home" at that early age was because my parents were concerned about my lack of confidence, shyness, dependence and fear of getting out to do things. I was so shy, I would hide behind my mother when the relatives and friends would come to visit us. I dreaded talking and mixing with people. My parents felt that the exposure in education in Australia would not just be a firm foundation but also help me get groomed to be a more confident outgoing person. The dream of every parent, especially an India Parent for their child.

Unleash the Fear:

At Nudgee College in Brisbane, I would still be stagnating when it came to unleash my fear and stepping up my confidence levels, until one day, one of my teachers taught me what and how to befriend my class mates, meet with their parents when they came to school on the weekend to meet their children and take them out.

Focus on Fundamentals:

Slowly but surely, at tortoise pace, I came out of my shell. I learnt the concept of mentorship and initially attached to one person called Uncle John and you will hear a lot more of Uncle John in my forthcoming book, *"Your Why! – The Driver"* Tagline - *"Destiny – Choice or Chance."* That initial breakthrough with Uncle John, and hundreds of other breakthroughs with my second coach Gerry, is what got me to becoming a Certified Practicing Accountant (CPA), and ultimately groomed to being the youngest VP for the third largest Oil & Gas corporation group.

Many would ask how from being an accountant to Coaching & Mentoring? My main trust of accounting was in this practice was off mergers and consolidation, and constant interaction with people of all echelons of management especially in a Start Up Phase. What happens when two companies merge? The culture of the company changes, the people mix within the company is changed, but it comes at a price, people disturbances and conflicts. We were asked by those companies to assist them in realigning their staff mindset and create a close to non- conflict zone within the office. It was through this that I expanded into training, development, coaching and mentoring.

Hence, I am stalwart when it comes to mastering and guiding people to unleash their potential. Do look out for our program "I-eXceL Wired For Success, and many other. These will be promoted on various platforms of social media. Check my company website ixlincorporated. com and my personal website davidnair.net

"My 10 Minutes" Purpose in Life Exercise

Sit in a quite spot and jot a few thoughts of what are some of the areas that you are very fond off and passionate about. When you think of them, a flame is kindled within you. What really fires you up when you speak about it with your friends. What fires you up, when you are on your own and you think about it, your minds run to places that you have never been before. It is as though you want more of it and not sure how you going to get it. Sit down and do not question these thoughts just jot them down, as the flow into you. What fires you up when you its spoken around you?

At the same time identify areas of limitations, that is holding you back and what would you like to do about it to scale yourself up from those limitations. Recall the three areas that I had personal gone through in my breakthroughs. What would you need to do to help you step me up?

As an example, I always cared for people, had a "soft spot for the underdog" as they would say in some cultures. I could not bear for them to be hurt. I would rush in there to want to help and give them a hand to lift them... Over time this evolved into my Definite Major Purpose. *"to create a Mind-set, Heart-set and Soul-set shift in 1 million minds, and their next generation, to stretch that little more in each of them, thereby contributing towards a better world for all of us and generations to come. "*

Chapter One

The Factor That Decides Your Success

Success is a state of Mind.

If you want success, start thinking of yourself as a success.

- Dr. Joyce Brothers

What does Success really mean to a person

Success is a subjective concept. It has different meanings to different people. To many people, it is large sums of money stashed away in the banks and material possessions. To others, it is enjoying good health or a high level of job satisfaction, or a feeling of deep contentment or happiness, or personal recognition for their achievements. Whatever your definition of success, this strong feeling of success must come from within you. Now, if "the within" is clogged up and lacks clarity, hence the flow and connectivity would be disrupted, then what do you think would be the outcome? That is one primary reason why many who set on working towards completing a task, a goal, a project, only a handful get anywhere close to achieving their expectation. Always understand no external forces could make you successful. **It is an inside out Phenomena.**

Your success in life is not determined by direct comparison with someone else, but by the accomplishment of an internally congruent aim or goal, the attainment of fame, wealth, or social status or, to some, the unconditional acceptance by everyone. It is vital to understand this term congruency – put bluntly "in sync". Let's explore this concept a little with the use of an android or I-phone. When we need to download or upload data, we connect cables between the phones and the laptop. For the download to be effective, the mobile equipment and the laptop must be in sync. Only then can data be transferred, otherwise no transfer will even happen. Similarly, for success. no data will be transferred down to the laptop. Why is this? The main reason being there is no connectivity between the equipment. Hence no matter how diligently hard one works at trying to achieve that goal, it always seems to flow past them leaving them disappointed. In addition to having this synchronicity in place one needs to also work at achieving that goal with resilience, determination, perseverance, and persistence to overcome the obstacles along that long, hard road to personal achievement.

"My 10 Minutes" **Empowering/Disempowering Barometer**

Stop here for a moment! Before we proceed any further, I would sincerely urge you take your notebook, sit in a quite spot for 10 minutes and pen a few points down.

1. What are the things that really make you feel great, happy, top of the world?
2. What are the things that really make you feel down, disgruntled, sad?

List them down. At this juncture please do not question, analyze what thoughts are coming into your mind. Just write them do as they pop in your mind. This is not the time to argue with your mind, analyze what is coming out of your mind or justify why it is coming in that manner. Instead the point of this exercise is to note down for 10 minutes the feel-good empowering factors and feel bad disempowering factors.

From this list over time, try and work on this disempowering factor. Look at ways on how you could reduce and eventually eliminate that disempowering factor. If help is required, drop us an email at support@ davidnair.net clearly indicating the disempowering factor and what have you done towards eliminating this concern.

The Gap Analysis

Have you ever wondered why some people become successful repeatedly, while others just cannot seem to figure it out? Let us say you take two people; you give both the same skills, the same opportunities and make sure that everything is equal between them, but only one person might succeed while the other fails. This is not really a hypothetical example. People do this all the time. A person sees that someone they know or admire is becoming successful by following a process, so they will try to replicate that person's results by following the same process. But does that guarantee, they will have the same results? In most cases No. So, what is the difference?

"*My 10 Minutes*" Gap Analysis

Take your notebook and reflect for a moment some of the people you know who successful and unsuccessful. Jot their names down and a few key points on each of them and what where their traits, their habits, behavior. How were they wired up? Do this for both the successful group and the less successful group. On a fresh page write some point about you and your traits, habits, and behavior patterns. If you were to measure them on a scale of 1 to 10 against those successful people listed, where would you rank yourself. What would you need to do to move up... Step up in life...?

From this list we recommend you work with the traits that had the lowest points. Work on trying to move it up by one point per month. This would take some effort, but when worked persistently you will see the benefits over time. Look at ways on how you could reduce and eventually eliminate that disempowering factor. If help is required, drop us an email at support@davidnair.net clearly indicating the trait you are working on and what have you done to stepping it up by one point per month.

Most Important Factor That Determines Whether a Person is Successful

Many hone-in and say: What is it that we need to do? What are the steps in doing what is required? How should we do it? When should we do it by?

Unfortunately, they are all correct and important but not vital. The steps are important to know and follow. But more important is your approach, your mindset, your attitude towards making it work. Are you genuinely happy doing what you are doing? Or Is it a chao, a pain in the butt so to speak? As an example, waking up on a Monday morning and growling, "Oh No, I must go to work. What a bore? My oh my, I have to put up with this person or that person etc." So where do we stand? How do we measure this? Happiness is an intangible commodity that is difficult to measure. But we could pull together elements that make and contribute towards determining whether a person is successful or not.

Now, to pacify the Melancholic, in this reading group, let me pen the specific steps towards working on achieving such an outcome. We crystalize this into a six-step process, with great emphasis placed on Step one. Why? Before we start on any journey we would need to know where we want to go. The remaining steps are disclosed briefly with some exercises and through the book with greater emphasis on all steps being worked though in the workshop.

Six Step Process for Success

1.   Know your outcome.

Let me ask you a question? How many have travelled in a train or a bus? Most would say yes to this response.... Do you know the destination of your travel before you leave your home? Do you know which direction you would head to board the bus? Do know what time the bus will get there? You will know what ticket to ask when you need to purchase the ticket. The answer to most of the above is in the affirmative.

My question to you is - **You have a life?** A fabulous life at that. Do you know where you are heading in Life? Have you personally mapped out the direction, the route changes, you will need to make, when you start and when you finish?

Hmmmm, I would suggestion you purchase another good notebook, call it your Dream Book, and start mapping your journey of your life. Create that blueprint of your life. You be that captain of your ship, directing and adjusting the sails as it makes its way through the seas, whether it smooth or rough seas, it does not matter. You will be able to steer through it when you have that blueprint well defined. You will hit a storm, but you will know how to navigate through that storm. In real life there are innumerable storms. It is how you bounce back, the speed at which you bounce back is what matters most. This is the measure of your resilience. Do not follow the process plant of life that is being mapped out by many, for many. Advice is cheap and be wary of where it is coming from. You will not source cardiac advice from a trade's person and in the same vein, you would not source trade advice from a cardiac surgeon. Go to the right source, heck it out and map out your blue print of Life, making it your Life of significance life, a life that you truly are proud to be linked to. A life that you will be remembered.

Now is the time to reflect what will your epitaph be when your friends and relatives are by you at the last moment. What would they say? How will they remember you? We will at I-eXceL - Wired For Success workshop go into this in greater detail helping you commence in building your blueprint of your life. We will at the next forthcoming book I-eXceL – Your Why? help you define your Definite Major Purpose, (DMP) in life. We will help you work through in understanding how to create a well-formed outcome - a simple seven step process. We will also challenge you and stretch you to have a portfolio of 100 dreams that you will want to work through prior to leaving this earth. Enjoy the start of this journey.

2. **Operate from a Physiology of Excellence.**

This term is been beaten around so often, what does it really mean?

Personal Excellence is **defined** as the ability to create solutions in difficult situations to enable yourself to overcome these situations successfully. In short, self-management that means "managing" your own mental and emotional state.

Therefore, the meaning of **Excellence is** greatness — the absolute best. **Achieving excellence is** never easy to **do. ... Excellence is** the quality of excelling, of being truly the best at something. To look at real life scenario a top student acquiring an A+ shows **excellence.** Another top student who has always been receiving a C, this time around receives a C+ or a B is also referred to as excellence.

Michael Jordan's basketball career was filled with **excellence.** When Michael started, he was not a top player. At every point that he scaled up the ladder to be the top player, he was exhibiting excellence through that journey. Its one's personal best in whatever they do. That is personal excellence.

Many would call out how do I work towards excellence. Are there any steps that I can follow, if so, what are they? We felt it best to walk through the steps with a real-life case that I had personally gone through with one of my participants....

From 2004, my company IXL Incorporated (www.ixlincorporated. com) was running numerous corporate development programs for about 30 of the high end MNC (Multi-National Corporations) in domains of Banking, IT, Pharma, Service Industries, Machinery,

Automotive and Hospitality. One such program we conducted was in Business Etiquette and Cross Culture Sensitization. This is for companies that are interacting, with clients from abroad or in a lot of cases the Indian executive is sent abroad to work with the client on their soil. This is to ensure whilst these executives are in the foreign location, their primary focus will be work, so they do not have to think twice about element that make up EQ – how and what to do there? Why? Because it has become second nature to them, and they can interact with ease and understand the nuances of that culture and do the right things.

This program is a 5-day hands on transformation development program. I am only addressing one exceedingly small minute segment here in this story.

The names here are fictious for the purposes here let us call them Ravi and Saris. One of the segments we emphasize a lot is politeness and the use of the three golden words of the English Dictionary – Please, Sorry and Thank You. It is one area where its use can help build Rapport, build Relationship, help mellow down discussion, lowers tone of incredibly angry people. Basically, its use does not in any way flame up a discussion – like throwing kerosene onto a fire.

These words do not come in as second nature whilst speaking, if used intermittently. In fact, I go so much as to tell the participants not to use these words, instead to abuse these words. Hence from the time they come to the program to the time they leave for abroad, they had to use these three words as often as possible – Massive Action!!!!!!till it's in their DNA.

In one of the batches that came to the training, there was a manager called Ravi who came to the program and was scheduled to leave for Durbin at the end of the month. He was a person who had the eye for detail and was one of the top performers in the team. So much so he used to go overboard in his practices, which from my perspective was fabulous. Following this segment each participate had to go home and use these three golden words as often as they can and share their experiences of what happened, the next day.

The first day Ravi goes home, sits for their dinner, and has a great meal. At the end of the meal Ravi gets up to wash his hands. On completing his hand wash, Ravi turns to see his wife who was by the stove boiling the night milk for their baby. Ravi looks at her and says Thank You for the beautiful meal. Saris was shocked at the comment and dropped the pot of hot milk on to the floor and without thinking she responds, we have been married for 18 years, and I have been cooking for you all that while and today you are saying Thank You. After 18 years. Stop for a moment and think, how many of us have taken a lot of what is done or said for granted. With no mention of Thank You or return of gratitude. Here Saris was totally shocked at the mention of the word Thank You. When a person is so devoid of appreciation, Love, Self-Image etc, they are like a person in the desert longing for a droplet of water to quench their thirst.

The next day Ravi comes to the program and shares his experience. He says to me David Sir, you are creating tension in my home. My response was simple – Ravi just continue doing it, trust me and see the difference in time. So, the second day Ravi on his way home he swings past a well branded, popular sweet shop called Ananda Bhavan. There Ravi picks up some Halva and other desserts for the family and rides his Hero Honda bike home. Just as he was entering his home, Saris comes out to greet Ravi, and he hands her this box of sweets. Saris look at the sweets and see the Halva, she cries out loud, places the sweet box by a table in the hall, and rushes to the neighbor's house howling – He is going abroad, He has seen a girl there and he is now giving me Halva. (For the foreign readers this a south India dig at a person, meaning you are going abroad, you found somebody there and now you are giving halva – the turf)

The next day Ravi shared his Halva story, and the group laughed about it and we continued with their diligent work on the other aspects of the program. Ravi went abroad, and I had never heard anything from him. About 3 months later, Ravi's wife Saris, sent me an email sharing her story.

She said, Mr. Nair you have not heard from me, but I am Ravi's Wife. In her mail she said Ravi was a very kind-hearted man and took care of my daughter and me. After your program, he began to care for me differently, he started saying I was good in certain things and could do other things better than his sisters and other friends' wife's. This boosted my confidence. I am writing this, so you could see where I was and where I have come to. I am uneducated, I come from a scheduled caste. I am from an extremely poor family; whose parents were farmers. I had extremely poor self-image and frightened to go out even to do the shopping. Ravi used to handle all that. After his encouragement, I would go out and do the household purchases, pay the utilities bills etc. I am now typing a letter (email) to you. It is my first mail. Mr. Nair, I said to Ravi, I wanted to do something so that I could contribute to the house expenses. Ravi's earns well, and he has always taken care of my daughter and me. He said we do not need that money, but when I said it make me feel better, he encouraged me to do this typing/secretarial course. Mr. Nair, I just wanted you to know.

I had not heard from either of them, for over 6 months, I then got another mail from Saris. Mr. Nair, I want you to know I have passed my secretarial course and got a job that is paying me Rs 8000 per month. Ravi said we will put that money into an account for our daughter and he will match Rs for Rs from his income for deposit into this account. We will keep this account for the education of my daughter.

About a year pass on I hear again from Saris, this time, Mr. Nair I found another job this is paying me Rs 18000 per month. Mr. Nair I never in my wildest imagination would have thought I could earn so much. Another year goes by and this time I receive another mail from Saris, where she indicated, that she got a promotion with the same firm and she was promoted as the personal assistant to the GM, and earning Rs 30000. She was so elated and over the moon. She then went into a lot of the challenges she had faced in growing up and this one success erases all those downers that she had gone through as a child. I was invited for a dinner with Ravi, Saris, and their child. A beautiful empowering family. At that dinner we laughed about the Dropping of the milk pot and the Halva story. She said it is amazing as she did not realize how much of potential, she has within herself. It was only when Ravi encouraged her and started being gratefully to her that she realized how much more valuable a person she was.

WOW! WOW! WOW! Is all I could say....

Friends you truly do not know how far that sign of care, affection, gratefulness would take you. Not just in the relationship, but in the build-up of your internal chemicals DOSE (Dopamine, Oxycontin, Serotonin, and Endorphin). I will not address this at this juncture but later.

"My 10 Minutes" Personal Excellence exercise

Stop here for a moment! before we proceed any further, I would sincerely urge you take your notebook, sit in a quite spot for 10 minutes and pen a few points down.

1. Ravi and Saris story journeyed through excellence covering the following key 8 steps. We would like you to identify the below mentioned eight steps in Ravi & Saris story.

2. We will also need you to identify a circumstance or situation in your life, where you had achieved excellence. Jot it down and identify through the below mentioned steps how your circle of excellence was achieved. Image that situation mentally a couple of time. Keep reimaging it consistently until its well anchored in you. Do this to such an extent that the anchored situation kicks in like an Auto Pilot and generates a feel-good factor. You be surprised how such simple shifts create massive gains in your lifestyle.

Key steps in attaining personal excellence.

1. Have the thirst or hunger for excellence. ...

2. Set your standard and Benchmark it against the best. ...

3. Have unshakable Belief that you can do it. ...

4. Strategize an action plan. ...

5. Roll model the best and be a student of them....

6. Remove all limits placed on yourself and just stretch. ...

7. Go all out, Work hard. ...

8. Focus your efforts.

Hereafter look at ways on how you are going to use these steps, to move up everything that you do by one notch. I mean everything. Take it slow and steady, inch by inch and see how much of a cinch it is to improve your performance. Look at your, many other successes and do the same practice in anchoring them as you did with the initial case above. If help is required, drop us an email at support@davidnair.net clearly detailing your query, and on the subject line please mark it as Personal Excellence – Ravi case or situation.

3. Have Personal Congruency

Many if they wanted something done would rush into the task of doing it like "a bull in a china store" without any thought given to mapping out what needs to be done, how it must be done and in what order it must be done. In addition, little thought is given to **The Flow**. Hmmm, opening another pandoras box. As many would have realized by now, thought is an electromagnetic wave its transmitted in that form, from one point to another. Just the same as a communication signal transmitted from a one phone to another. Now, with that in mind, when we add to it the traffic that is up in space, and the path that this thought travels through should be of least resistance for it to get to the destination. Without getting into details – as I said earlier a pandora box is opened on this subject and will not have the space to cover it here, instead will further elaborate it at the **I-eXceL – Wired For Success** workshop. But one thing that needs to be addressed is there should be synchronicity between the person doing the task and his mindset. The two should be aligned. Another example, when you are making a call and just as you pick your receiver you negate the call by saying "oh, I am sure they are not there", or "they are not going to pick the call" or some other negative thought. Guess what, that is exactly what the outcome would end up being... Now this is a hard call to continuously check our mindset as we keep doing so much and always in an environment that is not conducive or favorable to the flow of thought. Hence, personal congruence is the state in which a person's values and beliefs are consistent with the way he or she lives his or her life. Value congruence is the extent to which the individual can behave at work consistent with their own self- image. It is difficult to experience meaningfulness in our work if we are expected to behave in ways that are inconsistent with the highest values, we espouse to ourselves and others. A person to achieve self-actualization they must be in a state of congruence. This means that self-actualization occurs when a person's "ideal self" (i.e., who they would like to be) is congruent with their actual behavior (self-image).

4. Take Action

Very simply put – follow Niki Tag. "Just Do It". In gest let's not be playing the role of an engineer, in analyzing, reanalyzing, and reanalyzing to the point of being paralyzed with analysis, so much so, that we are paralyzed with analyses, that we do not move any further than analyzing

"My 10 Minutes" To do Action List

Stop here for a moment! before we proceed any further, I would sincerely urge you take your notebook, sit in a quite spot for 10 minutes and pen a few points down. Write down an exhaustive list of all the things you were planning to do, and wished you had done, and are doing into your notebook. Do not analyze these to do list, what to do, how to do when to do. Just jot down your list of items to do. Later we will come back to this list and prioritize it based on our Definite Major Purpose and so forth.

5. **Sensory Acuity**

Sensory acuity is an NLP (Neuro linguistic Programming) pattern that is used regularly in all sectors of our life. It is basically how we use our five Physiological sense of seeing, hearing, feeling (physically and emotionally), smelling and tasting. It is a vital to our existence. Knowing how to master Sensory Acuity will mean that you will ahead of the crowd when it comes to:

- Spotting opportunities
- Seeing the big picture
- Noticing what others do not (even though it may be in plain sight)
- Sensory Acuity is about seeing more of what is already there and training the brain to have a wider spectrum of vision.

Try this snap exercise:

- Without looking at your watch, can you describe it?
- What color is the face of the watch?
- Are the number roman numerals or ordinary?
- Do you have a second hand?
- Does it rotate smoothly, or does it glide?
- Is there a name written on the face?
- If so, is it in capitals?

You may look at your watch every day but not really know or take in much about it. Sensory Acuity is when you become aware of everything.

Sensory Acuity can further assist You by:

• Being present in the moment

• seeing reactions from other people when you talk to them

• Imagine how it will feel when you are even more observant and notice more.

• Imagine being given the inside information on how people operate and how to influence them!

Everything that goes into us mentally is through these five senses. Hence the passage should be free of blockages and it should be at the cutting edge to receive these inputs. If the input is filtered due to our past experiences, cultures, education and exposure then the information that is received into us, is not in its truest form, distorted, discolored, deleted and we end up working with this second-rate data. Hence our outcome too is of that quality....

Realizing this it is vital to ensure our five senses are at its cutting edge 24/7 for the full absorption. Hence what are we doing daily to have these senses at its cutting edge. Everyday how are we sharpening our senses.

"My 10 Minutes" Sensory Acuity

Stop here for a moment! before we proceed any further, I would sincerely urge you take your notebook, sit in a quite spot for 10 minutes and pen a few points down. List the five-sense explained in Sensory Acuity. Self-assess where are you on a scale of 1 to 10 on these senses. List down three situations where you had excelled in your performance because you were at the cutting edge with your senses. Do the same for three cases where you had missed out on your performance due to poor cutting-edge senses. The information received, filtered, and interrupted were way of off mark. Write down what was the cause of it and how you could improve on the performance the next time around.

6. **Have behavioral flexibility for mastery**

It is amazing what behavior, attitude and approach towards what you do has such a significant impact on how the outcome turns out. To illustrate this let me share with you this father (John), daughter (Sally) and wife (Suzie) story. It also encompasses what is commonly referred to as the 90/10 rule of Life. Picture how a perfectly fantastic day was messed up.

The 90 10 Rule

Put bluntly, the 90 10 Rule is where: In 10% of life, things happen to us we have no control over these events. While 90% of our life depends on how we react to the things that happen to us. For these we have total control over our choice of reaction to the things that happen to us.

Check this case on hand - Imagine at breakfast time in a normal suburban home, John and Suzie with their daughter Sally are sitting at the dining table. Sally turns around quickly to reach out for the Ipad, sitting on the bench. As she does that, she knocks her coffee all over her father John's white shirt.

Scenario 1)

John shouts and yells curses and says "What a clumsy thing to do Sally. Why did you have to reach out for the Ipad and not get up and go to the bench and pick it up. How could you be so clumsy! Now I have to go up and change into another shirt." John then shouts at his wife, saying it's your fault, "Why did you leave the coffee so close to the edge of the table!". He storms upstairs to change his shirt leaving behind a daughter in tears and a wife that is fuming.

John is leaving home 5 minutes later and the traffic has picked up. Sally is deeply hurt, grumpy, in the back of the car and totally ignoring him. John drops Sally at school, she is late as assembly had stated and she did not get a chance to talk with her friends prior to assembly. John eventually gets to office fuming, hot tempered and in a state of flux. His boss greets him and tells him "let's review that important document we need to deliver today". Suddenly John face went pale and realized in all that rush, he had left the notes on the table in the hallway, at home. He left it out their table to do a final review during breakfast, but with the chaos at home, that plan went for a toss out the window. Hence John went rushed out without going through the paper or even picking it up. His boss fumed out of his office, yelling at John go home and pick it up, as it is an important opportunity and a vital client. John returns home to pick up the document. The day proceed with one such mis hap after another... John was happy to get home and hit the sack.

That night the house is a tense angry situation with nobody talking to each other...

Why did John, Suzy and Sally have a bad day?

1) because of the spilt coffee?

2) because of Sally spilling the coffee.

3) because of the traffic?

4) because of his boss and the important meeting?

5) because of John's reaction to the spilt coffee?

Scenario 2)

In this case, although Sally spills the coffee and looks shocked and concerned. John looks at his shirt, pauses, and looks at his daughter and says, "Oh no I will have to change this shirt. Not to worry, I have another one upstairs. Sally in future you need to be a little more careful. It's only a shirt. Let me get upstairs and change my shirt and be down in a moment. John hugs Sally pats her on the head and goes and changes his shirt. John comes downstairs, by which time Suzie has Sally in her car taking Sally to school. This gives John a few minutes to glance through the document as planned. He refines the document, makes a couple of more additional notes, and gets into his car to drive to work. There is traffic, but John is control and focused on the way, running the document delivery in his mind. He is practicing the presentation out loud in the car. John arrives at work, goes to his office settles in and enters his boss's office. He delivers a well thought through effective presentation. That night he reaches the house, and everybody is sitting at dinner sharing their day, in a happy mood.

Same story, two different scenarios, they began the same but ended quite different. They ended different. The people are the same. Their approach, their attitude, their mindset, their level of EQ was all different. All because of How John chose to react to something that happened to him.

10% of life is stuff that happens to you. 90% depends on your choice of reaction to what has happened to you.

"My 10 Minutes" 90 - 10 Rule

Stop here for a moment! before we proceed any further, I would sincerely urge you take your notebook, sit in a quite spot for 10 minutes and pen a few points down. Write down 5 instances that you had gone through like what happened to John. These could be instances that you had encountered with your family, friends, or colleague. Pen these down in detail. Spend some time reflecting on what would have been a better option for you to have done such that the circumstance would have panned out a lot better than it did when you went through it.

The Tipping Point in Success

Small Shifts generate Big Gains

- davidnair

Let me share with you what really makes the difference when one person succeeds, and another fails? Many have friends who are school or college drops outs but have excelled in life. What makes the deference. I refer to it as the tipping point, the breakeven point. It is the biography of experiences that have tried many methods, patterns to succeed in life all condensed into a disciplined way of thinking, communicating and behavior. Its these small shifts that generate big gains. Once cemented, these contagious life patterns will use universal laws to anchor one success after another. Many sails past this phenomenon and live a life that is painfully average and mediocre. They struggle from month to month with their finances, from one relationship to other, not being able to nail the heart of the issue. Hence, they would not even experience the flip side of life. I would sincerely encourage our readers to research our "I-eXceL Wired For Success" development plan and do yourself a favor in registering for the next workshop that is near your city.

What Does a Mindset Determine?

The greatest discovery of my generation,
is that human beings can alter their lives,
by altering their attitudes of mind.

- William James

Your mindset is one of the most important assets that you have, and it plays a major part in the way you look at the world as it influences many things in your life. A mindset is like a window that you see the world through.

In a brief nutshell, everyone, through conditioning has established their own mental filtering system for processing the data that is absorbed through our senses. Our first mental map of the world is made up of internal images, sounds, tactile awareness, and internal sensations. Tastes and smells that is formed because of the established neurological filtering process, commonly referred to as the first mental map of the outside world.

Personal meaning is assigned to that information that is received from the world outside. We assign a language to that internal images, sounds, feelings, tastes and smells thus from our everyday conscious awareness. This second map is commonly referred to as the linguistic map – the luggage to which we refer to the original map of the outside world.

The subsequent behavioral that we exhibit, because of the neurological filtering process and the linguistic meaning we had given to that original map creates our programmed conditioning. This is what causes us to act and feel the way we do.

Now to alter this we work on the filtering system and cleanse it. We will in "I-eXceL - Wired For Success" spend time in going into the details on what to do, how to do and when to do the process of cleansing those filtering.

You can even say that if you had the right mindset; you would be successful even if all the other factors were fighting against you. Of course, that is not exactly the case because your mindset determines how and if you see opportunities when they come along!

My trigger for change happened when I was working for an Oil & Gas company as the VP for Finance and administration, with responsibilities for Administration, IT, HR, and Finance. I had a team of various levels of people reporting to me. I was constantly looking out for opportunities on how I could enhance the productivity of my team. We would send the teams to various development programs, seminars, and conventions to upgrade their skills.

It was during that phase, that I received a flyer promoting a program titled "Unleash your Power" by Tony Robbins. I had never heard of Tony Robbins. Two things that immediately caught my mind about this program and its promotion: the first being Key learnings covered in the two-day session were, how to turn fears and business challenges into power, the key to a quality life working with state change. The second, Tony was offering a table of ten for the price of nine attendees.

I mulled over for a while, whether I should go, the time, the cost and many other objections were coming to my mind. Today I know it is normal, thought process that a person does go through, when one wants to get out of one's comfort zone and do something outside that box thinking mindset, its normal to have such objections. It's an everyday happening.

How did I come out of this mindset? I did one thing that I have been advocating through my journey in developing people. I went and sat with a person earning an income that was many times greater than mine. Who could that person have been? He was my then boss, friend, and mentor – Gerry. I bounced the thought of attending this program of Tony Robbins with Gerry. In our discussion, he threw a few pros & cons of attending the event and went on to make a statement that had stuck in my mind. David if you did not go to this event what is changed in you to perform better tomorrow, the next day, the next week the next year. He went on to ask, would it be the same thing, you have been doing over the last few years?" My response was "probably Yes". He followed with a "Why"? I said, "because I had not acquired anything new to make that shift." He finished off by saying, *"Continue to do what you are doing now, and hope to gain a different result is commonly referred to as insanity."* I thought to myself "Wow". I came out of his office, and immediate got my assistant accountant to raise a voucher to book two tables (I could take part of my team to the event.) for Tony Robbins Seminar, "Unleash the Power within"

Many have been put through such similar situations of deciding for something or other. What is the first thing they do, ask their friends, neighbors, relatives etc. These spheres of influence are in most cases earning the same level of income, or a bit more than them, they have the same lifestyle or something a bit better, the have the same circle of friends, the same mindset etc. One cardinal rule I was taught very early in my life, if you had a cardiac issue and needed a heart surgery, who would we go to see? An accountant, a teacher, a cab driver, or a cardiac surgeon? The answer is obvious, a cardiac surgeon.

Then why is it when it comes to our life and where we are going in life, we are locked into seeking advice from our close and dear once? There is nothing wrong with our close and dear ones, they are there always there to help and support us, but when it comes to specific life journeys and decision to make out of the various available options, do we resort to people of our same level of income, wealth acquisition and lifestyle? The answer a resounding No.

There is a powerful well sought-after mentor to many of the teachers in the world of self- development named Jim Rohn. He puts it succinctly, show me five of your closest of associate, - friends, relatives that you hang out with, and I can tell you within a few hundred dollars what your material lifesavings are and where you are in the wealth continuum. So, friends just take stock... seek out the right advise form the right platform, and more importantly learn that good advice does not come free. Do not come with the mindset of seeking advice on Life transformation for free. You will not do that when you hire an accountant, an architect, a doctor or a neurosurgeon. Then why seek that from an Excellence Peak Transformational coach. To multiple the standard of your life many folds over, please consider the right source to acquire your advice and pay for it.

Now you may think changing your mindset is going to be difficult, but it isn't. Think of it sort of like mining coal. Once you can dig down deep and find out what your current mindset is, you will be able to change it (commonly referred to as introspection). The only hard part is getting past all those defenses and convincing yourself that you not only have the power to change your attitudes but that you have the responsibility as well, to yourself, the people around you, your circle of Influence, the community, and to those who are trying to help you be successful. There are a few basics commonly referred to as fundamentals, that you want to understand about mindsets so that you can have the best chance possible of changing yours and avoiding the pitfalls that plagued so many on this path. Let's discuss a few of these things, to keep it in mind.

It is Never Off - It's Always Working

The first thing that you need to understand about your mindset is that it is always on. No matter what you are doing, no matter where you are in the world and no matter how you may be currently feeling your mindset is still working, positively or negatively, for better for worse. What this means, of course, is that everything in your life is affected by your mindset. Even your family life is affected by your mindset. Everything such as - The way that you handle yourself with members of the opposite sex, the way that you present yourself to those you consider above or even below you, the way that you view yourself and the way that you view other people who have had success.

Let me tell you about Frank. He is a middle-aged office drone who has been looking into starting his own business online. He has researched some of the people who have been successful at various forms of Internet marketing and Frank thinks that the reason that he hasn't been able to be successful at it, is because they have more free time than he does, they had money to actually run their company and they were better informed when they started than he is. That is why Frank thinks that he is not successful. The truth is, Frank has not even tried one single Internet marketing method. Frank's mindset is that he is already at such a disadvantage that he might as well just give up before he even starts. The amazing thing is – Frank does not even realize that. - That is the problem.

Your Mindset - Conscious, Subconscious and Superconscious

You may not know it yet or believe it, but your mind consists of three aspects – the conscious, the subconscious, and the superconscious. These three levels of consciousness have different functions, and each has its own unique role in how you lead your life. If you want to achieve great things in your life, you must be able to harness the power of your superconscious mind.

Here lies the secret to the successes of famous people who are admired all over the world like Albert Einstein, Mozart, Bach, Leonardo DaVinci, and other distinguished scientists and artists.

The superconscious mind holds the key to the immense knowledge and information that you may be able to use to accomplish your goals.

The Conscious Mind

The conscious mind is the analytical and logical part of your brain. It analyses data based on your five senses of sight, touch, hearing, smell, and taste. The conscious mind can distinguish right from wrong, good from bad, up, or down, etc. Unfortunately, the conscious mind is limited in its capacity in terms of understanding and storage of your memories.

The Subconscious Mind

The subconscious mind is where all the personal experiences, emotions, beliefs, thoughts, and ideas are stored. You sometimes use your subconscious so you can function on "autopilot." For instance, you still know how to ride a bike even if years have passed when you last used it. Likewise, you know how to swim even if you have not practiced in a long while. This is because your subconscious has already stored the knowledge in your mind, and it's just a matter of accessing it.

The Superconscious Mind

There are different terms that describe the superconscious mind according to diverse beliefs, philosophies, religions, and spiritual teachings. It may be called the" infinite intelligence," "collective unconscious," "oversoul," "universal mind," The Source, Divine Mind, One Mind, or even God.

All the things that you want to know about the universe are stored in the superconscious (infinite wisdom). All this information and knowledge handed down through time can be accessed by everyone on the planet, provided the person knows how to retrieve it.

Another aspect of the superconscious is collective consciousness. This means that every person is connected to the mind of every other individual. It is highly possible to communicate with one another by just using the superconscious mind.

The superconscious is not bounded by any limitations or restrictions, thus anything that the mind can envision can be made into reality.

The Subconscious Mind and Superconscious Mind Connection

Your goals or desires are produced by your conscious mind. You can successfully achieve these goals by tapping into your superconscious mind, since all the information that you need is already available in this level of consciousness. However, you can only connect to your superconscious through the subconscious mind.

The subconscious can relay and accept wisdom from the superconscious. When this happens, everything falls into the right place. You can find suitable opportunities, helpful persons, conducive environment, etc. so you can be successful in your endeavors.

How do you access the superconscious mind through the subconscious mind? There are various ways by which you can do this. One is through practicing meditation. By relaxing your conscious mind and freeing your thoughts, you will be able to access your unconscious mind.

Another way is through hypnosis. A qualified hypnotherapist will be able to guide you through the process.

Practicing affirmations can also connect you to the superconscious. An affirmation is a positive statement, in the present tense with the pronoun

I. By repeated saying these statements/mantras whist in a "state" of great feeling has power in accelerating the manifestation of the required outcome. The power lies not in just affirmation, instead in the incantation - An **incantation** is a way of embodying the truth of a statement and involves a change in state and physiology. Find the power say only positive things to yourself and banish all negative thoughts.

Harnessing the power of your superconscious mind is the key to your success. Achieving your heart's desires are possible if you've the proper attitude and belief that you possess all the tools that you need to make them a reality.

In my next book I will be drilling down in into this area of Superconscious in greater detail.

Hmmmm, I had originally thought we would do a chapter on the interweave between the subconscious & super conscious mind but felt it would take away from the other areas that need to be covered for the I-eXceL Wired For Success. Hence that segment is differed to the next book. Nevertheless, what we going to do is ski through the surface of the topic of the subconscious mind, stopping at a few touch points and how we could utilise it for our rewiring and mastery of self-excellence.

The power of your Subconscious mind

The magic power of the subconscious mind is infinite. I have seen and personally experienced miracles that has happen to men and women in all walks of life all over the world, with the power in using their subconscious mind. This can happen to you too when you begin to Tap into this magically power.

Some basic introductory highlights of the sub conscious mind. Its mind makes no judgement. It will accept everything that we say and believe. Our sub conscious mind is our best ally, it loves us enough that it will give us what we declare. We have the choice and control on it. If we select poverty belief than it assumes that is what we want and will work towards providing it, as it assumes that is what we want. It will continue to provide us with those things until we change our thoughts, words and beliefs for the better. Interesting enough, our sub conscious mind does not know from true or false, right, or wrong. We do not want to talk ourselves down. We do not want to talk to ourselves like, 'Oh stupid, old me," Why? Because the sub conscious mind will pick that and deliver that to us – after some time you will feel that way. The sub conscious mind has no sense of humor; hence you cannot joke with it about yourself and think it will take it as a joke. It will take literally what is given or said to it and manifest it. At the I-eXceL - Wired For Success, workshop we will go into practical demonstrations to tap into this power, what it takes to be congruent with it, what we need to do to nurture it etc....Miracles will happen to you too. We have designed it such that, when you begin using the magic power of your subconscious mind, it will expose you into creating that life of significance

"My 10 Minutes" Conscious, Subconscious and Superconscious

Stop here for a moment! before we proceed any further, I would sincerely urge you take your notebook, sit in a quite spot for 10 minutes and pen a few points down. Write down your understanding of the conscious, sub- conscious and superconscious mind. What are areas that you feel you need to work on to get a better appreciation of these power houses within us.

Ever Considered Why These Differences Exist?

One man could be sad while another man happy?

One man could be joyous and prosperous while another man poor and miserable?

One man could be fearful and anxious while another full of faith and confidence?

One man has a beautiful, luxurious home while other lives in a meagre existence in a slum.

One man is a great success and another an abject failure?

One speaker is outstanding and immensely popular awhile another mediocre and unpopular?

One man is a genius in his work or profession, while another toils and moils all his life without doing or accomplishing anything worthwhile?

One man healed of a so-called incurable disease while another is not.

Why is it so many good, kind religious people suffer the tortures of the damned in their mind and body?

Why is it many immoral and irreligious people succeed and prosper and enjoy radiant health?

Why is one woman happily married and her sister very unhappy and frustrated?

Is there an *answer* to these questions?

A resounding YES and where might it be.

In the workings of your conscious and subconscious minds

One of my mentors John Grinder, the founder of NLP had this to say when I kept questioning him during my infant stage of understand and appreciating the power of the unconscious mind.

"David first make the unconscious mind your best ally, then work with it using the process that we had worked with you and after a while you will understand and appreciate the power it has to doing what you want done." I stuck to working with what John suggested and the results have been amazing. We will share this with you in greater detail at the workshop session.

Clean Your Window

> Better keep yourself clean and bright;
> You are the window through which
> You must see the World
>
> - George Bernard Shaw

On my first trip into India in 1998, I was advised by a few friends, if I wanted to get to know India, it would be best for me to walk wherever and whenever possible and at other times to use public transport instead of driving from point A to Point B. Hence for my first trip from Chennai to Pondicherry (a French colony south of Chennai) This journey commenced at the main intercity terminal at Koyambedu. A few minutes after I had boarded the bus and found my seat, I noticed a person, later found out he was the bus attended was perched on the bumper bar of the bus and peering into the bus from the front windscreen, he was wiping the windscreen with a crushed-up newspaper. He started the windscreen cleaning at the driver's side and finished at the passenger side of the windscreen. A few minutes later the driver hopped on the bus and we commenced our journey to Pondicherry. We travelled for about 1.5 hours and the bus stopped for a pit stop at Muttukadu (a mini lake on the outskirts of Chennai). Today a flourishing metropolis with various varieties of water sports for tourist and weekenders. At that spot the attendant again hopped on the front bumper bar to do the same exercise of cleaning the front windscreen. We subsequent continued our journey and proceeded to Pondicherry, arriving there 4.5 hrs later. It is interesting to note for a 4.5 hr travel, we had a 50-minute stop, and the windscreen of the bus was cleaned twice. Remember this, cleaned twice, in that short span.

Most of us have been exposed to computers. How does data, information get into a computer? Through the keyboard, external hard drive, pen drive, downloads etc... My question to you is how do we as human beings, receive and process data? Many would still be wondering how? That truly shows how much we know about ourselves? Who we are and How we operate? How we think? How does the processes inside of us click on and click off? Many have been having a roller coaster ride, leaving it to nature, to chance to just continue doing what they have been doing and hopefully in that course, we will flush this concept of understanding us as human beings.

Even more frightening, many are totally oblivious to the functioning of our mind and body. How and when should we do certain things to have maximum output. Take note, if we are owners of business, we source for outcomes through reports, performance, revenues, costs... If we are students, we measure our performance on how well we do our assignments, examinations etc. if we are in HR, performance is measured on how well we hire the right person for the right job for our organization, and on, and on, and on, an endless list.

The point of entry for information for us is our five senses: Visual, Auditory, Kinesthetic, Olfactory and Gastro. The first three are primary sense, whilst the last two are secondary senses. Of the primary, Visual sense is what we have been addressing so far.

As shared earlier, the windscreen was wiped twice for a 4.5-hour ride. My questions are, when did we last wipe, wash, or sharpen our vision like the attendant did to the windscreen of the bus. Many miss this finite point of continuously cleaning sharpening "the saw" for all our senses, in this situation it's our visual sense. As the image flows from the external world through to our internal world, it goes through multiple filters.

These filters are built over time and is based on the 3 E's - our education, experiences, and environment. ....

Hence the input of whatever is out there that our eyes captures, and what we see is not the true image. We have had a life of many years, when did we last clean our visuals.... If our cleaning is limited, how pure is the information, the image, the data that is coming into our brain via the eyes. Hence how are we interpretation this data. What will the outcome truly be? Many unanswered questions. Most of us have a mainstream education, a degree or two, in some cases a doctorate.... Hmmmm

On account of the altered image, the outcome of the individual's behavior because of such filters to is different - whether it's a behavior, a performance, mastery of an instrument, studying for examination, performance at work, it will all be impacted.

What is the solution – Simply put we need to regularly clean that windscreen How do we clean the wind screen? When do we clean the wind screen? What do we need to use to clean the windscreen?

Many are unaware of what needs to be done to continuously clean, to continuously sharpen the saw, and be at that cutting edge such that the true image can be seen in its original state, as it enters our eyes. – What it really looks like in the world out there.

The process for this cleaning, will be shared at the workshop detailed at the end of this book. The workshop you will be able to acquire a better understand, appreciation, learning and application of these elements of life

Everyone has this windscreen when they are born, all our windscreens will be untampered, hence the clarity through which we will see the world would be clear without any tint, or filter.

We all start with a clean window. We look at the world through these senses. During our journey through life of growing (I call it the process plant of making us what we are) we go through our sight and learn an enormously amount. Everything, we see, we soak it in, the good and the bad. We do not distinguish them. They are soaked into our system and remains there, creating the person we become.... as an illustration, look at a child that is beginning to walk. When the child stumbles and falls. What does the child do? Does the child frown do the child blame the carpet? Do the child point finger at his mother or father for giving the wrong instructions Does the child quit? The child just smiles, gets up again and makes another attempt and another, and another, and another... as many times as the child will need to do, to eventually walk.

There will come a point either through education, experience, or exposure, where rubbish is hurled at the child. The window gets splattered with criticism from everyone around that child – relative, friends, and teachers' parents. The window will get smeared by rejection, disappointments, doubt etc. It is unfortunate this dirt keeps building up, one layer on top of another layer, on top of another layer. This build up cause drop in enthusiasm and the string of negative emotions of depression, frustration, anger... in time they would give away on their dreams and life a non-exciting life with minimal or no achievement

You might think that you get a break from a destructive mindset when you are sleeping, but sadly, that is not the case. No matter if you're awake, asleep or somewhere in between, your mindset directly affects the kind of things that your subconscious mind tells you. If you have a negative mindset, your subconscious mind could be reinforcing negative attitudes at night while you are sleeping. Even your dreams could have an impact. Suppose deep inside, you do not really believe that you have the ability or power or skill or whatever it is that you believe you are lacking – to be successful in life. Until you change that mindset, you will be getting it from your mind when you are awake, when you are asleep, and pretty much always, for the rest of your life until you're dead. While you're unconscious your subconscious mind will be working overtime to plant seeds of doubt that will keep you from success.

"My 10 Minutes" Clean Your Window

Stop here for a moment! before we proceed any further, I would sincerely urge you take your notebook, sit in a quite spot for 10 minutes and pen a few points down. Identify three areas where you will need to work on yourself to clean the window of your life.

The Cost of Making Big Changes

Are you a smoker or have you ever been a smoker? If not, do you know someone who has? If you do, you might be aware that when people desire to quit smoking one of the biggest barriers that stand in their way is that they believe that they will be sacrificing something if they give up cigarettes. Their brain somehow convinces them that they are going to be giving up a huge part of themselves – a vital part of themselves – if they quit smoking. Of course, the truth is, that all the things that they'll be giving up such as poor health, difficulty breathing, increased risk for lung cancer and the rest, are all things that they want to give up anyway. They're not going to be giving up a part of themselves and all. In fact, they will be getting a part of themselves back.

But the mind is not an easy thing to convince. Défense mechanisms are built up, pathways in the brain are forged and that metaphorical wall is built, reinforced, and then surrounded by a dozen snarling Rottweilers. When you want to change, you must make it through these defenses and although it is doable, it is not going to be easy. But getting rid of the failure mindset and giving yourself the success mindset is worth it.

Your Inner Voice

The thoughts we choose, becomes the tools
we use to paint our tapestry of Life

- davidnair

How often have you heard that you could change your life if you are willing to change your thinking? More important your thoughts shape your future.

I had heard this many time but did not understand it nor its implications until I met with one of my mentors, John Grinder. It was then that I got the opportunity to discuss, brainstorm and grasp the concept of that place of intuition within us. – commonly referred to as the inner voice. Over the years, after repeated experiences, lots of learning, immersed me into this pattern for development in how we think? I eventually began to realize the impact it has and how significant it was in creating the required change by just changing how we are thinking and speak to ourselves. Now in all instance when this voice calls out, I just follow it... This does not come easy, but after repeated practice, and when congruence happens within oneself this intuition just unfolds. When you decide, mountains are moved for manifestation to occur.

While working through self-talk, I began to realize how much I self-criticized myself and I tried to stop it. I was also exposed to affirmation. So, I started repeating affirmations with the hope it will create a shift in my thinking.

Did It?

In a lot of cases it did not, so I used to question this concept. I used to hear John say, you will need to work on congruency. Never understood it. Until one day the tube light just shone. The internal environment and the externally environment need to be in Sync. Like download from a mobile phone on to a laptop, it only happens if there is synchronicity. I then started to work on myself and over time a lot more of I was being immersed in the concept and found the strike rate of success with it began to grow, This surly boast one's confidence. I could notice minor shifts and over time they the process became simpler, and simpler. I would practice this on simple things like having a straight run into work with red light, finding a park closest to the entrance of the shops that I went to. This was enough to boast one's self and say this thing is powerful and works. Inch by inch I slowly work in mastering this science of controlling my inner voice and continued using this concept on bigger and larger request to be manifested. it began to work...

Now I am the Voice.

I will LEAD, not follow.

I will BELIEVE, not doubt.

I will CREATE, not destroy.

I am a FORCE for Good.

I am a Leader. Defy the odds!

Set a new standard!

Step Up!

- Tony Robbins

"My 10 Minutes" Inner Voice

Stop here for a moment! before we proceed any further, I would sincerely urge you take your notebook, sit in a quite spot for 10 minutes and pen a few points down. For one full day write in bullet points what has your inner voice been telling you. - Empowering and Disempowering talk. Make a list of that and start working with those disempowering noises to look at why they are there and what are you going to do to get rid of them.

Hung By Your Tongue - Power of Spoken Words

What you say is what you manifest

- davidnair

We have all heard of the law of gravity. There are also laws in Physics, Electricity, Science and other domains. Similarly, there are spiritual laws like law of cause and effect – what you give is what you receive. There is the law of the mind. How does it work? I truly do not know. In the same way, I do not know how electricity works? I only know, if I need to have light, I flick the light switch, and guess what the light gets turned on. So, when it come to the laws of the mind, I am not a neurosurgeon to understand the internally processors that process the mind. All, I know is when I do something there is an outcome and this or that is the outcome.

It's been proven, thought is energy, an electromagnetic wave. It gets emitted into space and travels along bouncing off from one obstacle to other. In the same way, when we speak on a telephone, it gets released out into space, and that sound from the voice gets transmitted to the recipient. Similarly, when we think a thought, or when we speak a word, it travels to our mind, and returns with an experience, after it goes through that filter of education, experience and exposure that we had referred to previously. That is why we need to constantly cleanse our internal filters. This is akin to cleaning, compressing, defragmenting a computer to get maximum output. Similar then our filters are constantly kept clean through the various patterns, that we will address during the I-eXceL Wired For Success workshop.

We now can see the correlation between our mental and physical being. We also understand how our mind works and its creative ability could be enriched further or stifled by the filters within us. The thoughts travel at high speeds through our minds, so do words when released into space. Therefore, it is vital, not important to edit what we say. How by listening to what we say and not release anything out without first editing. The impulsive outburst that happen during emotional state. Yes, it is hard, but through constant practice it can be conquered. By so doing the amount of negative thinking influenced talk coming out of our mouths. Always remember there is tremendous power in the spoken word, it could make or break a relationship. So be mindful, start practicing thinking through what is being said before it spills out of the mouth.

Just as when we are constructing a building, a home, we need to lay the foundation, only then with the structure stand firm and withstand the storms or any natural calamity. Similarly, words are the foundation to all communication, to whatever we want to create in life. We constantly use it without giving a second thought, to what we are honestly saying and, in some instances, what we are truly saying? Most of us hardly pay any attention to what we are saying, to the selection of words. Due to environmental conditions – the people we associate with, has a huge influence on what we say and how we say it. Hence it goes with saying if they are into constant negative muddle, guess what, that is what we soak and release unknowingly due to our condition over time.

Grammar is taught in our English lessons and we were taught to select words based on the rules of grammar. These rules of grammar keep constantly changing. So, whatever was proper in the past could be improper now and vice versa. Idioms and slangs also change with time.

Unfortunately, grammar does not take into consideration the meaning of words or how it impacts our behavioral life's.

A time for us to take stock. Schools did not teach the choice of words you use and say, would have anything to do with the experience of life. No teacher mentioned that thoughts were creative and could shape your life & destiny. No mention what was spoken in form of words would return in form of experiences. I do hope this does explain a very basic fundamental creed of life. "do to other, as you would do to yourself." What is released out comes back to you. Did schools teach you, that you are worth loving, or that you deserve good. How many recalls as kids we would often call each other cruel and hurtful names and try to belittle on another? Why did we do that? Reflect for a moment. Where did we learn such mentality, talk and behavior? Was it from home, when some of our parents, called us stupid, laze or dumb? was it from friends who would feel powerful with bully words, you idiot, no one would want to go out with you, you ugly so and so. Some of us just cringed at those words. But did not realize that they were well imbedded into our subconscious minds and impacted our subsequent growth.

A powerful story of little Jonny comes to mind. Little Jonny had a very foul mouth, in that he always swore, spoke in foul, bad language. His parents were very annoyed and found it extremely embarrassing, when Jonny used to do it in the presence of relatives and friends. At the advice of some close friend, Jonny's dad got to working with Little Jonny. They lived out in the farm in central Queensland. So, his dad got little Jonny a toolbox with a hammer and a bunch of nails. The instructions were very simple, every time little Jonny said or used a bad word, he had to go out to the fence post and hammer a nail into the post starting This punishment was to start nailing every fence post from the front gate. This Jonny meticulously followed, as his mum and dad kept a mindful eye on him. Jonny would have hammered at least 100 nails over a three-week period. The parents also noticed during that time Jonny began to slowly stop saying foul words until one day went by when he did not say any foul word for the whole day. This went on for a week, until one day Jonny came up to his dad and proudly said, "Hi dad I have not sworn for over a week. His mum and Dad were proud of him and complemented him on his effort to change. His dad then said to little Jonny, what I would like you to do now that you have stopped using foul words is to go out and daily pull out one nail for every day you do not say a bad word. Some days went by and little Jonny came up to his dad in a perplexed voice said, "As I am pulling the nails out, I am leaving behind a hole where the nail was previously" His dad pulled little Jonny aside, sat him down and explained. That is what happens when you hurl hurt, aggression, anger, other disempowering emotions verbally. You leave behind a hole in the heart of the people you hurled that abuse. That scar will take a long time to be healed, sometimes it will never heal at all.

> **Be mindful of the power of your words and**
> **use it diligently and in a thoughtful manner**
>
> – davidnair

Watch Your Words and Blaze a Trail with Your Words

> **The words that you frame and**
> **say will shape your future.**
>
> – davidnair

How often do we seriously think about the words we use each day of our life? Are we careful in selecting them? Many would question why all that fuss with mere words? What is its significance to me? Each word that comes out of our mouth has that magnitude of power to manifest into reality without us realizing its being done. It can either build or destroy your future or strangely enough maintain status quo.

To put it succinctly This is what happens in the process of thinking and verbalizing:

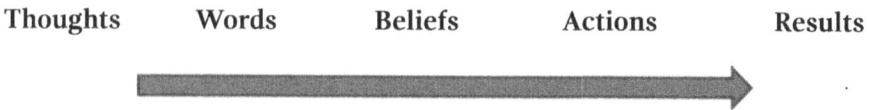

Thoughts	Words	Beliefs	Actions	Results

$$\longrightarrow$$

Let me elaborate this in a case that I worked with and experienced the transformed outcome, I am again using fictitious names.

In one of my flights from Chennai to Kuala Lumpur, I was on an aisle seat. Sitting next to me was a young kid about 10 years old playing with his game boy. Every so often he would lean forward and try to catch the eye of another kid sitting on the same row across the aisle but was by a window seat. After about 30 minutes into the flight I heard this voice from across the aisle calling out, excuse me sir, do you mind if I moved seats with the little boy sitting next to you so he could play with his cousin sitting here by the window. I said yes, no issues. They swapped seat and this young girl (Raji) sat next to me reading a magazine, whilst I continued reading my book. After a while Raji asked me what was the book I was reading? I responded, Intentions by Wayne Dwyer. Her response was Wow, what his perspective on Intentions? Long and short of our 4-hour flight talk – Raji was a gold medalist in her college, top performer in IT industry she worked at and was a top performer heading towards a spectacular career in the IT industry climbing the corporate ladder in leaps and bounds. Unfortunately, she came from a culture where she had to be married whilst she was in the mid 20's and she had to give up her career aspiration for taking care of the home, the family. This was a huge blow to Raji. Initially she went into a frenzy, and was uncertain what she had to do etc. Her elder sister was very supportive and caring, in fact, so much so that she paid for this trip from Raji, her nephew and an aunty. Raji, was meeting with her sister in Malaysia for a week vacation to help ease the pain that Raji was going through. She has been through numerous highs and lows during the last few months. The states of depression, that Raji was in and out was in no way helping with the finding a suitable suitor for her life. Everything that Raji was speaking about, the behavior she portrayed was coming from a victim standpoint of view. She was not allowed to do this or that, she was not good for anyone that is why the suitors that are put forth are not acceptable for an arranged marriage etc. Blame, blame, blame Syndrome. When we landed at KL Airport, I left her to meet with her sister and went my way to my connecting flight to Australia.

A few weeks later I had an email from Raji, seeking assistance. I reached out and worked on a few patterns for change in particular the language she uses. Started her on an affirmation then an incantation trail, and to be conscious of what came out of her mouth, what she spoke to herself when she was alone. Worked with her on several areas, commencing with her purpose, mental refocus, association power and slowly could observe a shift in happenings.

The suitors that came looked more favorably towards tying the knot. The shoe was on the other foot now, she was not a victim of circumstance instead, she was in control. The outcome of 8 months of intense self-work, especially on how she thought, and what she spoke. Raji found a very compatible partner in life ended up marrying that person.

On reflection Raji, had many times inferred how the change in her attitude, words that she selected thoughtfully before speaking had a dramatic impact on her way of life. She commented it was startling to see how what a changed person she ended up being just by changing what she thought and said. From being a very outward, energetic, enthusiastic person, prior to being pulled out of work. To the state of being at the lowest ebb of how she felt was devastating to say the least. Did this happen from saying, I am no good, nobody loves me, I am not going to find the partner of my life. This was reinforced further by the comments from the environment. Repeated saying by her relative, parents and friends further reinforced this fact. So much so that Raji believed she was not worthy of a partner in life. All this changed when she started working on herself, her thoughts, her affirmations assisted increasing the required switch. Many do not realize, how words affect our emotions, our beliefs, and our effectiveness in performance of life.

> **You are not what you think you are.**
> **But what you think – YOU ARE!**
>
> **– Dr Norman Vincent Peale**

"My 10 Minutes" Watch Your Words and Blaze a Trail with Your Words

Stop here for a moment! before we proceed any further, I would sincerely urge you take your notebook, sit in a quite spot for 10 minutes and pen a few points down. Keep a note for a week what have you been saying to people around you. Jot down the instance, what caused you to say what you said. Look at how better could you have handled that situation. What do you need to do to step up the game of what you saying to people or are you in a position where everything is fine and there is no course correction to make.

Chapter Two

Know You: Journey of Self-Discovery

Circumstances Uncontrollable

Thoughts Controllable

Who is in charge?

YOU

- davidnair

Dedicate Full Attention to Yourself

I can say with confidence that the moment a person truly starts down the path of self-discovery, they will never turn back. Many may ask the question, "What is self-discovery?"

The American English Dictionary defines self-discovery as follows:

"a person becoming aware of one's true potential, character, motives, etc."

So, let me start by asking you a few simple questions:

- What are the steps to self-discovery?
- To begin with, do you know yourself well?
- Are you clear about what you want in your life?
- Do you have a sense of purpose?
- What defines you?
- What makes you happy?

If you stop to reflect for a second, you may find yourself answering "no" or "don't really know" to most of the questions above.

Should this be true, you are not alone.

It may also be that while you are happy with some parts of your life, there could be also parts that you do not like. Not being happy overall with your life is an indication that are things unresolved.

Up till now, it is very possible that you have not gotten to know yourself very well. You have been running on the treadmill of life. A great proportion of your time has been spent on working long hours, slaving away in a job, and filling your days with back-to-back activities. Your mind is just too preoccupied with things to do.

Unfortunately, not knowing yourself well can result in an unfulfilling existence. Because when you have no clear idea about what your inner values, core beliefs and goals are, you are likely to allow your emotions and decisions to be externally dictated. Instead of making an independent decision, you adopt the values, core beliefs and opinions of your friends, colleagues, or parents, as your own. Thus, you would have no clue about what your personal boundaries are, even if they have been violated. While others can count on you for support, you are not sure that you can count on yourself.

In the journey to self-discovery, it is particularly important to understand what is success? In today's world, a good percentage of people define success as having lots of money in their bank account, being on the cover of magazines, becoming famous and so much more.

At every stage of our lives we grow, at every level we want something more and we keep feeling like there is an aspect of ourselves we have not harnessed or tapped into.

"*My 10 Minutes*" Full Attention on Myself and Answer These Questions

Stop here for a moment! before we proceed any further, I would sincerely urge you take your notebook, sit in a quite spot for 10 minutes and pen a few points down.

1. What feeling in your life do you seem to be pursuing?
2. What gets you out of bed in the morning?
3. What in your day gives you that warm feeling inside? As some would refer to it as The Buzz. Is there a way you could have it every day?
4. Does your current job/occupation/business allow you to fulfil your needs?

5. If we lived in a world with no money – and therefore no salaries – would you still be working in the same place, doing the same thing you are doing today? Why?

Now open the Pad again and look at what you wrote. Will that warm feeling be present in your future? Will you be doing tomorrow that which satisfies your needs?

If not, it is time to rethink your career business and life.

> **Choose a job you love,**
> **and you will never have to**
> **work a day in your life**
>
> **- Confucius**

At different points in time, success or being successful will mean different things to different people. Below are six key points to note during your journey to self-discovery and success.

Six key points for self-discovery and success

1. Success is transient: It is all about growth, awareness of where you are, where you are going and the ability to put in place milestones that would be used to measure your journey. Success is not a destination; you can never fully arrive at a place and say you are successful. Success through self-discovery is about understanding that one can never fully know himself or herself.

    Discovery of self is transient based on your environment, situation and circumstances, your vision, mission, purpose, and the resources you have. The revelation comes with your evolution – the more your change and are aware of the changes happening within you, the more you become.

2. Understanding Your Purpose and Identity: According to Charles Darwin, it is not the strongest of all species or the most intelligent that survives, but the most flexible.

    Therefore, our brain which is the control center of our body is designed in such a way that it is dynamic and flexible. Self-discovery deals with knowing and discovering yourself at every point you are in, understanding your purpose and the solutions you are created to provide.

Always bear in mind that you were created for a purpose. Once you can discover and push it, you can achieve so much.

Do refer to the segment on Defining your outcomes to map this out with better understanding

3. Understanding your History and Reality Check: Mapping reality requires that you understand your history and match it with your purpose.

    Everything you go through is instrumental to everything you will ever become, so there is need to accept and celebrate your history. Understand your root; learn the wisdom in it that relates to your future.

    Discover the mindset you developed as a result of your history, your core ideologies and philosophies you learnt; ask yourself questions and find out if where you are at each point is where you really want to be.

4. Sense of Self-worth and Self-confidence: This is fundamental for self-discovery and success. For a person to develop a healthy self-worth and self-judgment there is needing to fully understand and recognize what your strengths and weaknesses are and focus more on your strengths. A lot of individuals concentrate more on their weaknesses because it is called a 'weakness', unfortunately people fail to realize that every flaw is a strength and every strength can be a flaw.

    You need to understand that nothing is hindering you from succeeding but yourself. You must work for what you want and must contribute something for the change you seek. Until you accept your difference (uniqueness), your voice and constantly tell yourself that you are worthy, you can do nothing.

    It is important to note that the journey to self-discovery and relating it to success starts from you. You deserve to grow and flourish. You need to fill your mind with positivity.

5. Environment and Relationships: No man can live in isolation. With every step we take, we need the right relationships and

environment. The true effect of communication comes from the output it leads to.

In matters of relationship, it is extremely easy to notice that the type of reaction you give out to people consciously or unconsciously is the type of response you will receive.

In order to change the type of reaction you get from people around you, there is need to take a step back, do an inward search and discover the type of vibe you pass across to people.

It is also important to note that in self-discovery and success you must first identify who you are, why you are in an environment and what value you can add. Sometimes your environment doesn't necessarily mean the physical environment but the human beings that make up your space.

At some point your success might require that you to create an environment within your environment.

What do I mean? You need to be able to visualize your desired future, shut out the mental noise around you and create the environment that can push you towards achieving your goals. You need to create a healthy physical, mental, psychological, emotional, relational and spiritual environment.

6. Discover your Passion: Passion is that which drives you, it is something you can do for free as it aligns with your natural gift and talent; that which you can carry out effortlessly.

In pursuit of your dreams, there will be challenges, trials and tribulations. But discovering your passion, understanding who you are and why you are unique is a great milestone which can aid you to be the best that you desire to be.

Finally, ignorance is lack of self-confidence and self-awareness of yourself and your environment. To succeed, you need to understand and master the dynamics within your environment, be dedicated and stay committed to your purpose. To consistently succeed you need to be flexible in your thinking, behavior, and actions.

We will drill down in greater detail this subject of self-introspection, at the I-eXceL Wired For Success workshop. Refer to the back of this book for more details on the programs and how to access it for your benefit.

"My 10 Minutes" Self Discovery & Success

Stop here for a moment! before we proceed any further, I would sincerely urge you take your notebook, sit in a quite spot for 10 minutes and pen a few points down. Identify three key notes that you could jot down in each of the six areas mentioned above. Areas that you would need to drill down further for self-discovery.

The Attribute to Your Success is You

"My 10 Minutes" The attribute to your Success is YOU

Stop here for a moment! before we proceed any further, I would sincerely urge you take your notebook, sit in a quite spot for 10 minutes and pen a few points down.

The next thing that you are going to do is determine what sort of attributes the most successful people in the world have, or especially, the people that you admire. You are going to make a list of things the entrepreneurs, success business people or corporate executives (whichever category you fall into) must have in order to be successful. These can be both wide and specific depending on what your goals are. For example, they need to be good at whatever industry they are in and they are probably also going to want to be skilled in things like social networks, choosing products, building business relationships and marketing.

You are going to want to be as specific as you possibly can because at the end were going to compare that list with your list of strengths. By comparing these two lists we try to find how many and what strengths you already have, that can help you, be that success you have defined for yourself. The more things you list, the more things that you're going to discover are actually true about yourself. This exercise is not actually about finding all of the qualities that entrepreneurs, success business people or corporate executives need to succeed; it is about realizing that you already have the attributes that it takes to be successful. You do have the attributes that it takes to be successful. This is readily apparent, because you are reading this book. People that are interested in success or

66

aren't motivated to better themselves and reach their goals don't read such book on success. In fact, they tend to avoid the subject as much as possible because it reminds them of their failures.

To kick start you, here are some of the more apparent attributes just to get you started:

- Determination: you have the idea or attitude that you are going to succeed no matter what, or who stands in your way and no matter what obstacles you encounter.
- A Passion for Entrepreneurship: if you are not passionate about working for yourself and owning your own business, it can be almost impossible for you to be successful at it.
- Optimism: you are optimistic about the future. You believe that good things are in store for you and your outlook is almost always a glass half-full kind of mindset.
- Patience: you are willing to work over a long period of time to get the results that you want. You are not going to give up if it doesn't happen quickly.

Chapter Three

Navigate Through the Maze

**Obstacles cannot crush me. Every obstacle yields to stern resolve.
He who is fixed to a star does not change his mind.**

- Leonardo Da Vinci

Picture yourself running through a corn field. Would you know where the path between the corn shoots would be leading? On stopping if you looked left, right, or behind you be perplexed, wondering which direction would I need to go to get out of this maze field.

Life could be just the same. Many are overwhelmed with the things out there to do, the timeframe in which it has to be done, how will you do it, which item to start first and would you need to source some external help? Questions, questions, and more questions.

When you start on a holiday, do you know where you are going? Would you have mapped out a plan at least know the destination? Know what to take, how much money to carry with you, where you going to have your stops, endless list of items, some of these items were would have planned for months ahead. Hence have some clarity, on the direction and purpose of what we are doing and where we are heading? If I ask you the same question of Life, many based on my 3 decades of coaching and mentoring experience would find it impossible to fluently share their direction and purpose.

Why?

CLARITY

Hence a simple stepped process to walk through that Maze field.

A Four Simple Step Process to Navigate Through for Clarity

1. Life is Filled with Obstacles or is It Hurdles?

To many, life is filled with obstacles. I prefer to call it hurdles. Why? I see obstacle as a dead end, a wall that blocks, stops movement forward, whereas a hurdle, like a 100-meter hurdle race. One would glide over the hurdle to reach the finish line, on occasions you might clip the hurdle, so what you just continue the race, if you did fall at that hurdle clip, you get up and continue the race. Why? Your focus was on the finish line not on the obstacle. Many miss this point – what you focus is what you get? You want to complete the race, your focus is the end of the race, the finish line, not the obstacle. By so doing it is startling what and how the outcomes for the race maps out.

Experience has taught me that when we are moving towards a fresh dream, a new venture, or a heartfelt desire, there will always be hurdles. That is part of the equation.

So, why is it that we are so often surprised by the hurdles? Why do we get side-tracked? Why do we stop along the way? Why do we give up? Why do we agree with the pessimists around us and say, 'I was a fool to think it possible'?

If you have found yourself in that position, I have good news for you. While you are still breathing the air, let me tell you a simple thing; it is still never too late to pick up that dream again with a fresh view, new strategy and go for it again!

But there are a few important things that you must understand if you are ever going to fulfil the reason that you have been born.

Always remember to Shake the Dirt and Step forward, like this donkey

One evening a farmer's donkey fell down a deep well. The animal cried piteously all though the night and for hours the next morning. The farmer thought through the morning and discussed with some of his friends at the corner shop, where the men would usually gather to discuss the happening of the previous day and what the highlights in the newspaper are. The farmer tossed his concern of the fallen donkey to the group.

The neighbors and the farmer decide the donkey was too old and the well needed to be covered up. So, they proceed to meet mid-afternoon, to fill the well in and thereby hopeful put the donkey's cry for help to rest.

The group gathered at three pm, each with a shovel in their hand and proceed to shovel and began to shovel the dirt into the well.

As dirt was shoveled into the well, the donkey was crying out louder, and louder. Then suddenly, the cry of the donkey stopped. The farmer peaked over the well, to see the what had happened. To his amazement he was astonished to see the donkey with every shovel of dirt that fell on the donkey's back, the donkey was doing something different....He would shake off the dirt and take a few steps forward. He kept repeating this as dirt was shoveled down the well.

Pretty soon to everyone's amazement the donkey stepped up over the edge of the wall and totted off....

In Life too ... dirt will be shoveled at us. All kinds of dirt.... Now the trick is .... **role model the donkey,** shake it off and take a step forward, shake it off and take a step forward.... it is quite simple; we tend to complicate the simple to the difficult. Each of our troubles is a steppingstone. It does not matter how deep the well is, always remember, **never give up,** we can get out of trouble by just repeating the process.... Shake the dirt, step forward, Shake the Dirt, step forward.

Obstacles Can Crush You, Hurdles help glide you to your outcome. Hurdles will delay you, but they cannot crush you.

- davidnair

The only reason you will be crushed is if you start to believe its threats. Close your ears. Shut out your mind to any negative thoughts. Declare 'I will not be defeated, and I will not quit.' Shout out loud that 'Every hurdle that I come across will teach me a new lesson or a new skill that will position me for my next success.'

Approach each hurdle as your teacher and not as your opponent. If you approach your life as a student, you will always be prepared to learn the lesson that hurdle will teach. Ask yourself the question, 'What can I learn from this?' and nothing will phase you.

"My 10 Minutes" Shake and Step Forward

Sit and reflect what were some of the hurdles that you had encountered in your journey so far. Write them down. The look at what where ways in which you jump over the hurdle to get to where you wanted to go. How did you do it and what if any was the pain that you had felt.

Hurdles Cannot Crush You

Hurdles may delay you, but they cannot crush you.

The only reason you will be crushed is if you start to believe its threats. Close your ears. Shut out your mind to any negative thoughts. Declare 'I will not be defeated, and I will not quit.' Shout out loud that 'Every obstacle that I come across will teach me a new lesson or a new skill that will position me for my next success.'

Approach each obstacle as your teacher and not as your opponent. If you approach your life as a student, you will always be prepared to learn the lesson that obstacles teach. Ask yourself the question, 'What can I learn from this?' and nothing will phase you.

2. Hurdles Lead to Stern Resolve

Something happens to you on the inside when people say that you can't. I have experienced this feeling time and time again with each crazy new venture that I have undertaken throughout my life.

It takes a stern resolve to push through the pain barrier, the opposition, the disbelief, the questioning, the doubt, the fear, the lack of resources, and every hurdle that is standing between you and the fulfilment of your dream.

This is where you step up a gear into overdrive. This is where you get creative. This is where you get imaginative. This is where you get sharper. This is where you kick over from amateur to professional. This is where your light rises above the pack and you start to stand out above the crowd called mediocrity. This is where you step up from being an under achiever and are transformed into an over achiever.

Steel is implanted into your backbone. Your eyes are transfixed towards your goal, and your resolve moves from a state of instability into a state of stern resolve.

"My 10 Minutes" Hurdles Lead to Stern Resolve

Write down situations and circumstances that you had to take a stern step on yourself, when people said you cannot do something. Write down what you did? How did you combat that conflict? In the end how did you feel?

Now treasure that feeling. Every time you get into such a situation, fall back on this anchor, and pull yourself. We will cover more of this in our workshop.

3. Keep Fixed to Your Star

Sailors in ages past used the stars to guide them through all weathers upon the vast oceans that they sailed. Because of that they reached their destination.

"My 10 Minutes" Keep Fixed to your Star

- What is your dream?
- What is your goal?
- What is your life goal?
- For what purpose have you been born?
- What do you wish to be remembered for?
- What legacy do you wish to leave?
- What imprint do you wish to plant upon earth for all eternity?
- What do you wish to contribute?
- What is your star?

It must be bigger than yourself.

I read recently that rich people who fail to share their wealth generally commit suicide or die a lonely death. So, it is very clear that we must live for more than just our own personal gain and comfort.

What is your star?

What will empower you to face obstacles, to learn from them, and to move forever forward to your destination?

4. Do Not Change Your Mind

Whenever an obstacle stands in your way it is so easy to convince yourself that it must have been a mistake. So, you change your mind.

I am as guilty as the next person to have yielded to this throughout my life. But it is never too late to get back on track.

Once you know that obstacles cannot crush you, that it has led you to a stern resolve in your heart and mind – a knowledge that you know because you know what to do with your life – and you are fixed to your star, then don't change your mind.

Stick with it. Improve. Learn. Grow. Go. Persist. Persevere. Never, never quit. Do not give up. You can do it. You will make it.

"My 10 Minutes" Don't Change Your Mind

Ask yourself this question. 'How long am I willing to push ahead through every obstacle I face until I see victory?' Write it down the obstacles. If your answer is 'forever', then ask yourself the question, What and why is an obstacle here, if I am committed and wanting success. Work on that obstacle. Look at what alternatives are available, to remove that obstacle. It has no place if you are committed to waiting for that set outcome – that set success. Hence that obstacle will bow on its knee. It will yield into oblivion. It will buckle under pressure applied by such a determined life. Try this out on obstacles as they come forward towards you. Chip at it one at a time and see how you progress.

Like the river that cut through the rock and formed the Grand Canyon, so too you will turn every obstacle into wondrous opportunities that will bring joy to not only you, but also to those who are impacted by your tenacity to fulfil the purpose for which you were born.

In Pursuit of Excellence

What is different about how High achievers drive in their pursuit for excellence? Whether their background is from Sport, Business, Career or whatever, they are have one underline fundamental in every nerve fiber. Their desire, their passion, their purpose, and their drive to be the best. How is this achieved?

A Few Basic Traits That Drive High Achievers

The approach everything Step by Step.

The set their next reasonable goal, just prior to achieving their current goal.

Each success leads to the next.

Each time they visualize where they want to be, what kind of person they want to become.

The approach their goal with the end in mind

The know exactly where they want to go, and they focus on that. As they reach that goal, a bit more confidence is attained.

They are not afraid to ask for help. Ask anybody anything. When they meet one Goal

Nothing Would Stop Them from Having That Hunger and Thirst to Be the Best

Purpose, Passion, Drive and Excellence

Great Minds have Purpose, others have wishes

- davidnair

Basically, There Are Two Categories

Everything we do, and everyone we are, is created by our purpose and values. Your values are what makes you tick. It is the source of your wants and desires. Most people neglect thinking about values. This is the starting block to trigger you to think about your purpose. It is what fuels your passion that drives for excellence. This tripod is the hub, the reservoir for our wants in life, it also is the source of who we think we are

In this area, I would boldly claim there are two categories of people: one group who have a purpose in life and the other group of people who are purposeless. How do I make this claim, simple after putting through 200500+ people through various program and our seminars?

The group that is purpose driven, has a different aura around them. They are at a high peak state, energized, an empowering behavior, with a can-do mindset and the list is endless, whilst those on the other spectrum of the continuum are totally the opposite. Now it's interesting to also comment here like attracts like, hence those with empowering states seem to have all the luck. Whatever they put their minds to it or not, they seem to achieve it compared to the other group.

My extension of the acronym LUCK is Labor Under Correct Knowledge.... It is this knowledge that I am referring to. the knowledge of behavioral science, the power of tapping within and manifest whatever they had as their objective to achieve. Luck plays into their hand in the right way.

**A man without a purpose is
like a ship without a rudder.**

- Thomas Carlyle

Look at the people with a definitive major purpose: - Gandhi, Churchill, JFK, Golda Meir, Martin Luther King Jr, Thomas Edison, Henry Ford, Margaret Thatcher, Chris Everett, Maya Angilou, and an endless list. These hero's & heroines come from all walks of life. You do not have to be famous person to live your life in a heroic way. Working through the patterns that we are covering in this book will put you in an auto pilot mode to achieve what is expected of a person from a peak state of being. I personally have been through this – without a purpose and with a purpose. I am telling you its far better, easier, and less stressful to drive through life with a Definite Major Purpose, than without one.

As I had mentioned earlier my purpose simply put: *"to create a Mind-set, Heart-set and Soul-set shift in 1 million minds, and their next generation, to stretch that little more in each of them, thereby contributing towards a better world for all of us and generations to come. "*

Hence while I am working in some countries where there is no power, roads are bad, rationed water, these do not seem to bother me. Why? They are not in my forebrain, instead my DMP is what is driving me. Because of the purpose, shift and I mean sometimes unexpected shifts happen. Why because I am not bogged down with the Pain, instead I am uplifted because of the gain and uplifted multi fold. The universe seems to collaborate with you and unfolds the unexpected.

"My 10 Minutes" Purpose, Passion, Drive and Excellence

Stop here for a moment! before we proceed any further, I would sincerely urge you take your notebook, sit in a quite spot for 10 minutes and pen a few points down. Stop and think for a moment, what is Purpose, Passion, Drive to you? Jot a few points on this before we proceed. Take it one step further and start developing your Why, Your Purpose? For being on this earth. What do you like you epitaph to say, when you leave this world? This is just the starting point; it will evolve it in time.

For me it is - Purpose, Passion and Drive collectively can simply be summed up as the direction and intensity of one's effort.

The direction of effort relates to whether an individual seeks out, approaches or is attracted to certain situations. For example, an injured athlete might be motivated to seek a physiotherapist's advice or a businesswoman to start an aerobics program.

Intensity of effort refers to how much effort an individual puts forth in a particular situation. For example, a weightlifter may train with friends 4 days of the week yet differ from them in the tremendous effort or intensity he/she puts into each work out.

Purpose, Passion and Drive could be referred to as Motivation. It is one of the most powerful forces that propel individuals and teams to achieve their goals. Motivation is the foundation of all achievements. In the absence of motivation even the most talented athlete may never reach his or her potential. The beauty of motivation is that it can be developed and enhanced on a consistent basis through the techniques employed by Inspiring Excellence.

If you want something bad enough, you can achieve it. To reach your goals, you need to be motivated. But self-motivation is not easy. It is built on what I call the ARCO Principle – Accountability, Responsibility, Commitment and Ownership.

What is Self-Motivation/Drive?

Self-motivation is having the drive and enthusiasm to achieve something without the supervision or influence of others. You take matters into your own hands, completing the tasks you are presented with. It is most certainly not a black and white concept; it is far from simple.

When you are more self-motivated, you feel more accomplished, reaching your goals. It is a great skill to have, as it can dramatically improve your quality of life. Once you understand the power of self-motivation, you can positively change many aspects of your life. It plays a huge role in Business, Career and Life development.

Find Out What Motivates/Drives You

No matter how strong your Definite Major Purpose is, there would be times when it quivers. Hence its prudent to understand what are the elements that contribute towards a person drive and motivation.

A catch cry I work, as an anchor – *"If your Purpose is Big enough, the facts don't count."* When your purpose is solid, strong, and consolidated it is set in Cement. What we chase as goals becomes the teasers to ensure your Purpose is missile locked to its destination. We commonly refer to this as aligning our goals to our purpose. Interesting enough when the alignment is in sync, it is surprising how the goals tend to be easily manifested.

Why?

The flow of energy is in one direction, towards its attainment. Synchronicity is intact. Hence less conflict, displeasures stress, disagreement etc, within oneself. The internal person is harmonized – he/she is in harmony with the external environment. Therefore, happiness is attained. This is the trigger for the holistic person attainment of Self actualization (Maslow's Hierarchy of needs). That is Happiness. Now you see how goals are manifested easily.

This may seem obvious, but we are not always conscious of what motivates us. Our motivations change throughout our life. As our needs change, our goals change as well. There are two types of motivation:

1. *Extrinsic*: This motivates people due to a reward or because it must be done. This may be for money, good grades, or power.
2. *Intrinsic*: This motivation is based on love and passion. It is something that you would do for fun, your personal interest, or a personal challenge.

We are all motivated by different things, which change throughout the course of our lives. Most tasks throughout life have a combination of both motivators. For example, one individual may be working solely to pay their mortgage, having no satisfaction. This would be pure extrinsic motivation. Another individual may love their work, feeling highly satisfied. Their house is paid off, and they buy what they want when they want. This would be pure intrinsic motivation.

Most people fall somewhere in the middle. They need to work to gain money, but they do feel a sense of fulfilment. Although most of us work for money, we still feel job satisfaction or enjoy the social aspect of our career.

Five Easy Steps to Help Reach Your Goals

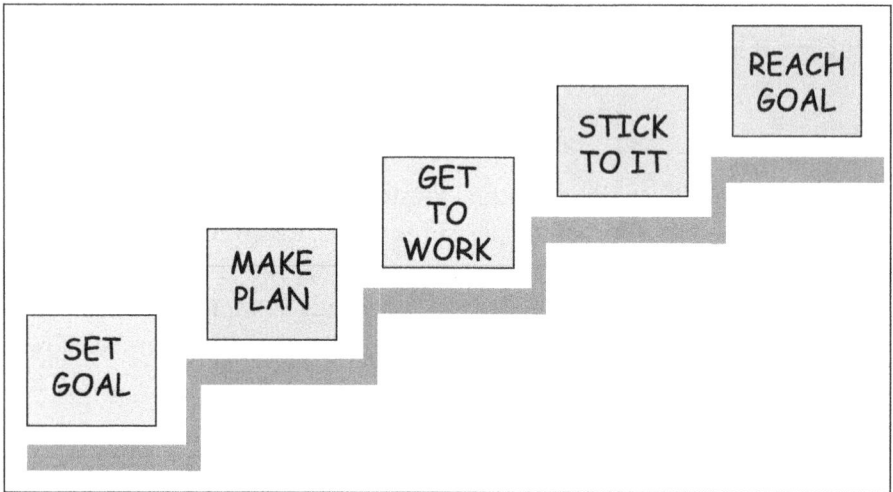

Many set their desires and wishes as PSEUDO GOALS. This is one primary reason why many of the pseudo goals are not manifested by a large percentage of people.

They are playing with their wishes and desires hoping it will manifest into a goal. Desires and wishes would become strong when supported by the 5 D's – Direction, Dedication, Determination, Discipline and Deadlines.

When you combine these five elements with the ARCO person (described in a later chapter) you are now cooking with gas. Manifestation of goals become easy. Many would go as far as to say it is LUCK. These people have luck with them and that is why they are achieving their goals. Little do they realize that luck is basically Labor Under Correct Knowledge. That is why I have always said this adage – You make your Luck..

When goals are set in alignment with your purpose you will be surprised how passionate you will be with the things you do. All task, I am referring to those associated with the goal achievement and other tasks that needs to be done which are not related to achieving the goals. The way you do these activities would be different. Your whole chemistry of performing the activity changes. You will constantly yearn and long to keep doing those activities, therefore the outcome too is stepped up. This build up our moral, self-confidence, self-esteem etc. Can you see the Domino Effect? The whole paradigm shift... from activity, task, goal driven to purpose driven.

Our goals are important but not vital in terms of the direction we take, the way we spend our time, and the resources we use. When goals are set, it's easier to measure your progress. Keeping your goals defined and current, is the best and most powerful way to keep yourself motivated.

If you put your priorities in check, and it is in alignment, there is no reason why you cannot achieve the life goals and dreams. If you look back at the age of 50, perhaps you will no longer be a figure skater. If that was your dream since the age of 10, you could have reached your goals if you put your plan to action. If you are self-motivated and the goal is achievable, there is nothing stopping you.

Once you choose your goals, you can then create an action plan. How do you plan to reach those goals? You want to be a nurse? Okay, start writing out your action plan. What education do you need? Who do you need to speak to? Are there apprenticeship programs available? Use the resources available to you. Do not look back and think 'I wish I did that.' You were able to all along. If you were self-motivated, you would exhaust all resources. Self-motivation and hard work will allow you to reach any goal.

When choosing your goals use the Smart Technique:

1. **Make your goal specific**

   S is for SPECIFIC. This will allow you to know exactly what it is you are moving towards. For example: I want to publish a book in the next two years.

2. **Make your goal measurable**

   M is for MEASURABLE. That way you can see the progress that is being made. In terms of publishing a book, break it down into deadlines. Next month you may approach various authors, getting advice. You will want to have your storyline completed, and the first chapter written. Once this is achieved, you can check it off. What is next? Move towards your next deadline. This will help you stay on track. It will also keep your motivation levels up.

3. **Do not make your goals impossible?**

   A is for ATTAINABLE. Make sure you can reach your goals. Each sub-goal may take a lot of effort, but you should know that they are possible. Millions of books have been published. This is something that is highly attainable. If you are weary of the publication process, that does not mean it is not attainable. You need to reach out, ask for help if needed.

4. **Create relevant sub goals**

   R is for RELEVANT. You will more than likely need to reach multiple sub-goals to reach your main objective. Make sure each goal is relevant to the final goal and to your life. The obvious sub-goals would be writing the content for your book. But there are also other relevant goals to keep in mind. Do your research, speak to experts in the field, and keep yourself motivated and determined. When you stay on course with your pre-planned goals, relevancy will not be an issue.

5. **Set deadlines**

   T is for TIME BOUND. You need to set deadlines and timeframes for each goal. Once again, you need to be realistic, but you also need to push yourself. If you have a set date in mind to complete sub-goal one, you can maintain a high level of motivation without being overwhelmed. Once that sub-goal is achieved, you are one step closer.

Once again, you may need to do some research. Maybe you are writing about current farming practices? You could use the first three months to interview people in the industry, get yourself out there and gain real-life perspective. Write out a timeline and cross off each objective. If you find that you are moving too slowly, either reassess your timeline or push yourself even harder.

"My 10 Minutes" Easy Steps to Reach Your Goals

Stop here for a moment! before we proceed any further, I would sincerely urge you take your notebook, sit in a quite spot for 10 minutes and pen a few points down. List down 3 of the goals you have been trying to achieve. Using the five steps process detailed above development you will use to lock down that goal you wrote above.

Excellence & Stress

Something is stressful only if you view it as stressful, accept it as stressful, and experience it as stressful. Otherwise, it is just something that happens during your day, week, or life. You can choose to feel stressed about it or choose to not feel stressed about it. Choosing to not feel stressed about things that previously resulted in you feeling stressed is within your potential control. You are not required to feel stressed before going into major events, competitions, tests, games, or performances. The best way to avoid feeling stressed in situations that previously resulted in you feeling stressed is to remind yourself that you are not required to be stressed in this situation. Remind yourself to keep things in perspective and then focus on following a positive preperformance focus plan that keeps you focused on you and what you can do in this context or performance. Focus on slow, relaxed breathing and remind yourself to *relax* as you breathe out in the lead-up time to your performance, test, game, or competition. Slow, relaxed breathing is always a good thing to focus on to relax or turn down the intensity in potentially stressful circumstances or contexts.

Changing channels is another effective way to reduce stress or regain control quickly on-site in performance contexts or other potentially stressful situations. Think of it as changing channels on your TV. If you are on a mental channel you don't like or don't want to be on at this time, a channel that is not helping you, simply press your thumb hard against your first or second finger and change channels mentally. As you press your thumb hard against your finger, think to yourself *change channels, change channels* from stressed to relaxed, from negative to positive, from distracted to fully connected. By choosing to make positive shifts in your focus, you can enhance your positive perspective; make your focus stronger, better, more consistent, or more complete; eliminate doubts or fears; and relax your breathing. All of this can help you channel your positive energy and fully connected focus into the step-by-step process of executing your performance to the best of your ability.

Another effective refocusing strategy I have used with high-performance entrepreneur, businesspeople and other high-level performers is called flowing stream. If you are feeling stressed or distracted before a performance or while you are performing, you simply imagine yourself flowing like a little mountain stream. If you watch water flowing down a mountain stream, you will see that it always finds a path even when there are obstacles like rocks, stones, branches, or tree trunks along the way. The water does not get stressed out or stop flowing; it just finds its own path and keeps on flowing to its desired destination. Sometimes it is helpful to remind yourself to flow through challenges, obstacles, or uncertainty in your day or life like a flowing stream.

My NLP exposure with John Grinder allowed me to further master the concept of Excellence through some of the patterns explained here. I have devoted much of my life to creating simple, positive, effective focusing and refocusing strategies to help young executives, business owners entrepreneurs and everyday people reduce stress, enhance relaxation, achieve their goals, and live their lives more fully and joyfully.

Your first line of stress prevention, stress reduction, and positive focus control lies in focusing on the good things in your life and accepting that your value as a human being remains intact regardless of whether you meet your performance expectations or the expectations of others. This is the prime reason why I introduce you to work on developing Your Why, Your Definite Major Purpose, especially if it is contribution in nature. These triggers the DOSE (Dopamine, Oxycontin, Serotine, Endorphins) chemicals within your body. is startling what happiness factor these chemicals can contribute to you.

In addition, the concept of You reducing unnecessary stress in your life by setting realistic performance goals, focusing fully on executing your task, and knowing in your heart and soul that you remain a good and valued person regardless of your performance outcome in any context on any given day. Choose to enter potentially stress-provoking situations with a positive and fully connected focus, and you will greatly enhance your chances of performing well. You may feel your heart thumping or a rush of adrenaline flowing through your body because you are excited, and you need a certain level of positive intensity to perform your best in this situation. That is usually a good thing because your body and mind are telling you that you are ready to rise to this challenge.

In some contexts, you may feel more of an adrenaline rush than you would like. If this happens, take a little time-out to breathe in and out slowly and remind yourself to relax every time you breathe out. If you are feeling negative or stressed, ask yourself:

Why am I feeling negative?

Why am I feeling stressed out?

What am I thinking or saying to myself about this situation that is making me feel negative or stressed?

Do I have to feel this way? No, you do not have to feel this way!

Do I have to think this way? No, you do not have to think that way!

Do I have to get stressed out over this? No, you do not!

Is worrying or being stressed going to help me in this situation? No, it is not going to help you!

Is it worth continuing to be stressed or negative about this? Definitely not!

If being stressed or negative is not going to help you, then why not change channels or shift your focus to something positive that will free you to take control and focus fully on performing your best? Set a personal goal to stop focusing on the negatives and start focusing on the positives.

- Focus on why you can achieve your goal.
- Focus on how you will achieve your goal.
- Act on your positive intentions every day simply by focusing on what you know works best for you. Continue to look for good reasons to believe in yourself and your capacity to meet or overcome the challenges you are facing, whatever they may be. You are fully capable of focusing through these challenges and growing from them.
- Remind yourself of your strengths. Write them down!
- Remind yourself to focus fully on the step, move, stroke, or stride in front of you and nothing else.
- Remind yourself of the amazing power of your fully connected focus.
- Remember that you are fully capable of achieving your goals.

- Remember that you are fully capable of carrying a positive and fully connected focus for the duration of your performance.

- Choose to think and act in positive ways that will free you to focus fully on executing your mission or performance - nothing more, nothing less.

Deciding to be positive and fully focused before you enter your performance context will help you make the positive changes you are seeking. Think about how you would prefer to respond to various situations in your performance arena and other arenas of your life. See yourself responding effectively to situations that may have distracted or upset you unnecessarily in the past. Imagine yourself in future performance situations - thinking, focusing, believing, and acting in more positive and fully connected ways. Focus on bringing this more positive vision of yourself to life in your real-world performance contexts.

Often a simple shift in focus from negative to positive or from disconnected to fully connected leads to a major change in the way you view a situation, your performance, and yourself. As soon as you start to believe that you really do have the potential to do what you really want to do in this performance context, everything changes:

Hey, I'm ready to do this; I can do this; I want to do this; I own my best focus; I control my actions and reactions; just focus, focus, focus, and execute my game plan.

Continue to act on drawing out the focusing lessons from your best performances and the less than best parts of your performances. Whenever you can make a positive change in your focus, perspective, or performance, think about what you did, focused on, or said to yourself to make this happen. Embrace those positive lessons and act on them in your future performances. Try to become aware of self-imposed obstacles to positive change, such as focusing on the negatives, dwelling on distractions, or saying things to yourself that block your own progress, as an example:

I don't feel ready; this will never work; I can't do this; I'm not good enough to do this; I'll probably mess it up.

What are you saying to yourself right now about your capacity to improve your focus and make the positive changes you need to make to consistently perform to your capacity? This is a good place to start establishing and nurturing a powerful, positive, fully connected focus.

Decide right now to move forward each day with a powerful, positive, and fully connected focus.

"My 10 Minutes" Excellence & Stress

Stop here for a moment! before we proceed any further, I would sincerely urge you take your notebook, sit in a quite spot for 10 minutes and pen a few points down. List down five stress situations that you would have encountered. For one of the identified situations, write out an action plane for stepping out of stress.

Excellence & Confidence Building

Confidence and self-love are critical aspects of yourself that needs to be developed because without them, you will always settle for less than you can have and deserve in life. You do not want that for yourself.

While I continue to stress the importance of confidence and explain some of the ways our mind works so you will better be able to harness the power of your mind, I want to make sure you get techniques and strategies.

Meditation is one way that will help you develop confidence and self-esteem. I recommend it as a life-long practice. Yet sometimes you just need something a little stronger. Something fast that has a lot of impact.

That would be the Circle of Excellence. The Circle of Excellence is an NLP technique that I love to use in my practice. The premise of NLP, or Neuro Linguistics Programming is that we each have all the resources we need inside of us. We just need to learn to tap into them.

We are born with one voice, one mind that is connected to the universe and source of all abundance and information. As we start being told we cannot do things, we are wrong and we are not good enough to do things, the second voice of doubt emerges and becomes loud and overbearing. Through NLP, you are gathering information from your subconscious mind. The mind that uses your original sweet, pure voice of truth.

In the Circle of Excellence, we will get into a state of confidence, certainty, and pride, then anchor that state. By anchoring it, we will be able to access that strong emotion when in a situation where we need that attitude to get the results we desire.

How well this works for you depends on your imagination and how well you can intensify your feelings. The actual application and practice of doing the Circle of Excellence will be covered at the I-eXceL Wired For Success workshop, which will be held in a city close to you. For this virtual Demo, just remember, pretend is your friend!

In this case, confidence is the feeling we are going for so I will pattern my example around that.

1. Imagine a circle on the floor in front of you. Make sure it is big enough for you to step into. Think of it like a spotlight shining on the floor in front of you.
2. Relax and clear your thoughts. Take several deep breathes.
3. Imagine a time when you felt confident and pretend it is happening now. Or even pretend you are in a scenario where you have a big project you just completed or a presentation you just gave. You know it is awesome, you were awesome, life is awesome, and you feel good. You worked hard, prepared and you crushed it! You feel good about the work you put it and it was easier than you thought. You have mastered a new skill and are ready for your next challenge. You are unstoppable. You knew you could, and you did it! And you did a great job. Everyone is so impressed with you. You are proud of this accomplishment and know you have earned it. All your efforts paid off in a big way. Can you feel the pride welling inside you? Notice how you are standing a little taller. You realize you are smiling from ear to ear. You have a peaceful calm washing over your stomach and there is a warm glow in your chest, filling your lungs with each breath you take.
4. Look at the imaginary circle and project the power of those thoughts, the energy and vibrancy into circle.
5. Notice what color the light is. Does it shimmer, is it moving? Are there sounds, perhaps taste or smell?
6. While noticing the color and texture of the circle of light, make sure you are sending all that confidence, love, and certainty into the light. When it feels so incredible you just must step in, then go ahead and jump right in.
7. Feel how this energy soaks into your skin. Breathe in that high vibration and healing. Allow the purity of light into your soul. Feel every cell in your body tingling with vibrant energy. Feel the confidence, the pride. Enjoy the certainty

8. Anchor that state with a word or gesture. For example, if you choose the word yes (a high energy word), make sure you say it with excitement and enthusiasm. It should be more like YESSSSS!!!!!!! If you select a gesture such as raising your arms in victory while tilting your head back while saying yes, make it a strong movement that is filled with the power of the energy you are harnessing.

9. Before the feeling fades, step out of the circle and shake it off. Ask yourself if you smell popcorn (a state break) and resume your normal state.

10. Repeat a few times if you like to lock in the state.

11. In the future, you can imagine that circle and just by stepping into it, you will feel more confident, certain, and good about yourself and life.

12. Alternately, you can also repeat the phrase or gesture you anchored in to achieve the state of confidence you need.

I am dedicated to making sure we raise to be confident, successful people who appreciate themselves as well as the possibilities and gifts life has offered them. I always like to remind myself that the best way to teach is by example, which is why we will all need to be role models for others to follow and implement these strategies.

"My 10 Minutes" Excellence & Confidence

Stop here for a moment! before we proceed any further, I would sincerely urge you take your notebook, sit in a quite spot for 10 minutes and pen a few points down. Rewrite the process in your own words. Practice this for the next 30 days. See how confidence is rebuilt.

Excellence and Affirmation and a Step Up to Incantations

There is a saying I have loved for years. The original thoughts came from Aristotle and were repackaged as we know them now by a writer named Will Durant. The quote says:

"We are what we repeatedly do. Excellence, then, is not an act, but a habit."

The quote is amazing, and I agree with it 100%. But today I want to focus more on the beginning sentence: we are what we repeatedly do.

I have been toying with daily affirmations lately. For the longest time, when I would hear people talk about affirmations, I would cringe a little inside. Thinking about someone standing in front of a mirror chanting something at themselves seemed a little odd to me. It was a strange practice because it was so foreign to me.

But then I broke it down and I realized I had often practiced my own version of daily affirmations without even knowing it.

I would give myself a pep talk in the car on the way to a business meeting I was nervous about. I would repeat positive quotes and phrases to myself before grabbing the mic to speak to a crowd. I was practicing daily affirmations but in a looser form, and that is completely acceptable. There is no hard and fast way to do them. There is no set of rules that says they must be chanted in a mirror or contain certain phrases. But so what if they are?

Let's say you look yourself in the mirror each day and say, "You are amazing exactly as you are and you are going to go out there and kick some ass today."

I cannot find a single negative thing that would happen as a result. Only positives. You repeat that day after day, and it forces you to approach the day and yourself in a positive manner. And after a while, you might even start to believe every word you say.

We are what we repeatedly do. If we repeatedly speak to ourselves in this uplifting manner, if we repeatedly talk in positives, that becomes who we are. Those positive thoughts are where our mind will dwell and will uplift us. Seems to me that mirror talk was NOT the odd practice I once thought it to be, but an amazing practice I wanted to implement. I wanted to be more intentional with my affirmations once I realized how much of an impact they could make.

Basically, an Affirmation is a positive statement in the present tense with a pronoun "I"

Examples:

I am a positive thinking person with a positive mental attitude.

I am a dynamic leader.

I am effective speaker...

So how do you go about doing that? How do you repeatedly implement these affirmations, so they become who you are? There are 3 easy steps I have taken to do just that.

Make them a habit: They call them daily affirmations for a reason. They must be done every single day. It could be first thing in the morning, while you are drinking your coffee and rubbing sleep from your eyes. It could be on your morning commute. It could be in the shower. It could be right before you step into the office. Wherever, whenever. Just make sure you do them every. single. day.

Make them matter to you: What are your goals? Your affirmations should back them up. This could be on a personal level or professional level. If you are struggling with self-confidence, make your daily affirmations positive self-talk—a few small words can do wonders to boost self-esteem. If you are focusing on overcoming fears, make your affirmations directed right at banishing them. If you are working towards building a life by your design, create your affirmations to back that goal up.

Make them your own: Want to chant at yourself in the mirror? Do it. Want to write your affirmation on your fridge so you repeat it every time you open it? Get it done. Want to give yourself a daily pep talk while you are still lying in bed, head on the pillow, gearing up for the day? Make it happen.

Your daily affirmations are just that. Yours. There are plenty of pre-written affirmations out there if you need a boost, but I've found if they matter to me, if I make them mine and if I repeat them every day, they do wonders to set the tone for my day.

Then look out world. I am repeating that positive conscious thought day after day, so it looks like this girl is on a one-way track to excellence!!

Affirmation is a powerful technique that has helped thousands of people achieve what they desire in life. Many people practice affirmations, but not every one of them manages to enjoy the fruits of it.

Scott Adams, the famous cartoonist behind Dilbert said that he used to write down his goals and affirmations. Every day, he would write down, "I, Scott Adams will become a successful cartoonist", 15 times a day.

And this affirmation technique has helped him manifest his dreams and transformed him into a successful cartoonist.

Affirmations work, just like goal setting and visualization. If you are practicing it but you did not see the results in your life, you are probably doing something wrong.

Here Are 5 Simple Steps to Make Sure That Your Affirmations Will Work for You:

1. *You Must Feel It*

   You must 'feel' your affirmations. Most people get it wrong because they are doing it for the sake of doing it. They do not associate any feeling or emotion into their affirmations. Therefore, their affirmations did not work for them.

   Therefore, include positive feeling words into your affirmations. For example, instead of saying, "I am earning millions of dollars every year", say "I am happily earning millions of dollars every year", and then feel the joy within.

   You can clench your fist, say it with power and as you mean it, and feel the energy flowing in you. When you feel the emotions, your affirmations will become more powerful and effective. You will be able to better program what you desire into your subconscious mind.

   It does not matter what affirmations you are practicing, when you include feelings into them, you can better manifest them.

   I am a powerhouse; I am indestructible.

   - Carmen Harra

2. *Repetition Is the Mother of Skill*

   Success will never come to you in an instant nor will you achieve the big results by taking just one step. The same principle applies to affirmation, you have to practice it every day to make it real.

   Do not just do it once and then forget about it. Scott Adams wrote down his affirmations 15 times a day and he did it every day, consistently. You must do the same.

How do you become good at something? Simple, you practice it daily. You do it each day until it becomes your habit. And when your affirmations become your deeply rooted habits, this is when you will start seeing the results you desire.

Most people don't have the commitment and they just practice it for just a few days hoping to see results. If you are serious about achieving extraordinary results in your life, you must commit to doing it each day.

Successful people like Michael Jackson, Warren Buffett, and Michael Phelps train to perfect their skills every day, and this is what you need to do with your affirmations too.

3. *Turn It into Your Habit*

If you want to maximize the effects of affirmation, you must turn it into your habit. Meaning, you must practice it at the same time every day. It is just like brushing your teeth each morning, you do it the same way and you will never miss out doing it.

The best time to practice your affirmations is once in the morning right after you wake up and once before you sleep at night. You want to fill your day with greatness by doing your affirmations. Set your pace right and start each day strong.

Also do it again before you sleep at night. When we sleep, our subconscious mind did not. You want your subconscious mind to continuc working with what you want in life.

4. *Believe That It Will Happen*

This is where most people get it wrong. They do their affirmations, but they do not honestly believe that they are going to get what they affirm. Just ask yourself this question, would you buy lottery tickets if you did not believe that you will win? No, you simply will not.

When you do not believe in something, you will never put in your full effort to do it. You will never act. When you believe that you are absolutely going to achieve it, you will do whatever it takes to get it.

Your beliefs define your actions. If you practice affirmations but your actions are not consistent with what you desire, you know that something is not right. And most of the time, it has something to do with your belief system.

So, choose to believe in your affirmations. Sometimes things will look bleak, but if you choose to believe in it, things will turn out differently.

You are a unique beautiful soul.

- Louise Hay

5. *Commitment and Action*

Finally, do not just practice your affirmations for the sake of doing it. You must put in your commitment to achieve what you desire.

If your affirmation is to have a slim body, be committed and take action to working out and exercising. Like I said, do not just say it, you must do it to show your commitment and that you truly believe in it.

Be determined with your affirmations because they work. Practice it daily. Do it at least once in the morning and once at night before you sleep. You can also include your affirmations in the mid-day to keep yourself driven and purposeful again.

Mistakes Made with Affirmations:

In my early days of working with affirmation, we used to do it in groups. A friend of mine who was big on daily affirmations and positive self-talk. He used to spend a few minutes every morning looking in a mirror and repeating, "I'm great. I am awesome. I'm a superstar."

He says his daily affirmations work for him, but his approach has always left me a little flat. Why? There is no action involved in his affirmations. He is great...but what is he going to *do* with that greatness?

Achievement is based on specific actions, not on general thoughts. The same is true of how we treat people: to others, we are what we *do*, not what we think.

And most importantly, genuine "success" means different things to different people. For some, it is money; for others, it is power and influence; for others, it is the strength of relationships. Your definition of success and what it means to you is what matters.

Therefore, the power in affirmation is the choice of the right words. Its need to be actionable words.

To help further guide you through in developing effective Affirmations, let us run through further samples, before we step up to incantations

1. **"I treat others the way they want to be treated."**

   By treating others the way, they want to be treated, my own personal fulfilment grows. I give respect and provide service. I show love, care, compassion, and consideration. I help others feel appreciated. I let others know they are important, that they matter, and that they are valuable. By valuing others, my confidence increases.

2. **"I am ever grateful."**

   Gratitude allows happiness to come into my life. I choose to show appreciation for what I have, whom I know, what I can learn, and whom I can help. I define and talk about the things I am grateful for daily. I know that the No. 1 way for me to be happy is to choose to be grateful. The more thanks I show, the more my confidence increases.

3. **"I am accountable."**

   I am reliable. I am responsible. I never blame others. I never make excuses. I take ownership of my successes as well as my mistakes. I know that my own performance is a direct result of what I think and the actions I take. By taking full responsibility daily, my confidence increases.

4. **"I believe in myself."**

   When I fail, I learn. My failures are temporary because my perseverance is permanent. I always push forward because I know I can succeed. As I continually believe in myself, my confidence increases.

5. **"I have high standards."**

   I do not let mediocrity enter my life. I am honest. I do not apologize for striving for excellence. My quality of life reflects my high standards. I rise and lift others with me. By living up to my personal high standards, my confidence increases.

6. **"I follow my heart."**

Time is precious, and everyone has something that they are passionate about. I do what makes me and those around me happy. The cost of not following my heart is too great, I am going to live life with no regrets. As I follow my heart, my confidence increases.

7. **"I trust my gut."**

I value my intuition since it is based on my subconscious mind and conscious mind working in harmony. I know what is true, and I know what I want to be true. I trust my gut feelings, my inner voice. As I trust myself, my confidence increases.

8. **"I am resilient."**

I have overcome many challenges and will overcome many more. The times that are the toughest are the times I learn the most. I never back down. I work hard and I push through. As I act in a resilient manner, my confidence increases.

9. **"I help people."**

I matter because I make a difference. While I may get tired, I am not weary. I share myself and love to serve. By making a difference, my confidence increases.

If we tell ourselves our personal truth enough, it manifests into reality. Our reality and our actions will always match the story we believe.

Incantation

An incantation is different from an affirmation, which is usually a repetition of statements, as shown above in one's head. An incantation is a way of embodying the truth of a statement and involves a change in state and physiology.

If you observe in the last 9 affirmations the statement embodied substance and truth. What we need to add to that is a STATE CHANGE and a power-pact impactful physiology shift It will have to be heavily action breathing with hand gesture, loud voice thumping of fist chest out and voice thrown out.. High energy.

One powerful incantation used by Tony Robbins is :

"God's wealth is circulating in my Life. His wealth flows to me in avalanches of abundance. All my needs, desires and goals are met instantaneously because I am one with God and God is everything."

"My 10 Minutes" Excellence & Confidence

Stop here for a moment! before we proceed any further, I would sincerely urge you take your notebook, sit in a quite spot for 10 minutes and pen a few points down. List down five areas that you would like to improve. Write out affirmation for each of the areas. Practice the affirmation. Rewrite the process in your own words. During you morning self-time, commence reciting your affirmation for Warm up with affirmations for one week. Then progress on to doing Incantation as described above. Continuous do this for the rest of your life. You will change the affirmation as the old affirmation is materialized. Commence again by rewriting a new set of affirmations. See how confidence is rebuilt.

Chapter Four

Developing the Self Right Framework (SRF)

**There is nothing either good or bad,
But thinking makes it so.**

- William Shakespeare

We have walked you through the fact that your Mindset is the vital factor in achieving success. You must have also identified key empowering and disempowering traits that you could work with in achieving the required success you had set for yourself.

So where do you go from there?

The very next step is to start by putting yourself on the path to healthy mindset habits. What is it? Habits are a funny thing though. Your habits are things that you do without even thinking about them. It second nature, its auto pilot mode of operating, with you realizing what you are doing. Each morning (hopefully), you get up, you brush your teeth and take a shower. You do these things without thinking too much about them. You are in Auto Pilot mode. You can be worried about something at work, dwelling on a personal issue or even deeply engrossed in a great novel and the subconscious part of your brain will still nudge you every morning until you have jumped in the shower and brushed your teeth or completed whatever your morning routine you have.

So, it is obvious that habits are one of your biggest assets when it comes to being successful. The people who are successful in this world are the ones who have developed the right habits. They do not have to think about doing things that make them successful; they just get up every morning and act, which of course, gives them the results that they want in the long run.

In this chapter were going to discuss how you can create habits that will allow you to change your mindset from a negative, self-destructive one to a healthy mindset that is ready for success.

"My 10 Minutes" What Do You Currently Do When You Get Up of a Morning?

Stop here for a moment! before we proceed any further, I would sincerely urge you take your notebook, sit in a quite spot for 10 minutes and pen a few points down. List down all the things that you do from the moment you get up. Its personal to you and you are not going to share this with anyone. So be comfortable and write it out. Be honest with yourself. We are going to do a Gap Analysis of the before and after. As we go through you will then write new patterns that we would recommend for you to do and without question repeat that exercise for 90 Days. Do not evaluate it and analyze the work in the initial 90 days. Just Do It. We will look at where you are after 60 days then after 90 days. Go into my You tube video under the playlist of Testimonials listen to a video by JP He was initially skeptical, but after 45 days he could see what was happening. So, trust the process. And Just Do It as Niki would say.

Start Your Day with Positive Affirmations

Have you heard the term self-talk? Self-talk could be more accurately described as internal memo-ign, or the constant communication between your conscious mind and your subconscious mind. For people who are not having success, and in fact, are having problems, negative self-talk is likely the reason why. Their subconscious is telling their conscious mind all these negative things and that just reinforces the idea that they are not successful and are never going to be successful.

You are going to do something different. You are going to wake up each day and give yourself positive affirmations. You have probably heard of these before and you may think they are silly. That is perfectly okay to think that they are silly, but still do them because silly-sounding or not, positive affirmations in particular Incantations does work. Remember that your subconscious mind is like a sponge. It soaks up information and then informs beliefs which then drive your thoughts and your thoughts control your actions. If you change a belief with positive affirmations, you will be changing your actions as well.

Find a place where you can actually say your positive affirmations to yourself, where no one will overhear you and where it is something specific and meaningful that will say to your subconscious mind: "Hey!

Pay attention!" For example, some people stand in front of a mirror, so they can look themselves in the eye and say their affirmations. Some people want as much privacy as possible, so they do it in their car on the way to work. It does not matter how you do it, if you pick a place and a time that is meaningful to you and do it every day. Create a routine that will develop into a solid habit.

"My 10 Minutes" Develop Your Affirmation

Stop here for a moment! before we proceed any further, I would sincerely urge you take your notebook, sit in a quite spot for 10 minutes and pen a few points down. Just as what we did for the confidence area, expand on your list of affirmation to encompass other areas for improvement and achievement of goals.

Spend Time with Your Feelings

When you do have doubts, try spending some time with yourself and taking a good, hard look at those feelings, to see where they are coming from. As mentioned, your behaviors today are the result of your thoughts which come directly from your beliefs. That means, if you are convinced that you're going to fail, which you might be if you haven't been able to attain success so far, then that belief is what is driving all those other factors that is keeping you from success.

"My 10 Minutes" Feelings Practice

Stop here for a moment! before we proceed any further, I would sincerely urge you take your notebook, sit in a quite spot for 10 minutes and pen a few points down on the following. What you can do, is when these doubts enter your mind, and you start thinking about all the ways that this could possibly go wrong, take a step back, and evaluate where the thoughts are coming from. Write them down. Remember, just because your subconscious believes something to be true does not mean it is. So rather than trying to push away these negative thoughts or avoid them, accept them. Now pen down ways how you could work to eradicate them by finding out which belief is driving them, where did it originate from and what is holding you back from moving forward. Pen these down. Review these talks to your subconscious mind and over time with continuous note taking and review look at the outcome. Ensure as you progress through this exercise, develop Incantation to practice daily and watch the results unfold.

Spend Each Day Learning Something New

You should never stop learning. No matter how much you know, there is always room for more information. Just as science discovers that the more that we figure out about the world around us in the universe, the more we realize that we do not know; It works the same way with your learning as well. Spend a little time each day learning something new that is going to help you.

You could read a motivational book. There are many different ones out there that are geared towards entrepreneurs and are written to give great advice from experts who have made a success out of entrepreneurship. Get on to my website to see recommendation of books to read. You can follow David Nair on Good Reads where he recommends books that you could read. You can find them at your local library or online in digital format. Books by Anthony Robbins, Stephen R. Covey, Dale Carnegie, and Napoleon Hill are all great reads if you're trying to motivate yourself and become more successful. There are many other places that you can find motivation. Go on YouTube during your free time and look for motivational videos if that's more your style or you could even correspond via email with someone who is more successful than you, who could be your mentor of sorts.

No matter how you get information, the point is, to keep learning and to devote some time each day to that learning. You do not even necessarily have to read motivational or self-help books. You could do something that improves yourself like learning a new language or teaching yourself a new skill, or by studying a subject that you been interested in, relating to your business.

"My 10 Minutes" Spend Each Day Learning Something New CANI Practice

Stop here for a moment! before we proceed any further, I would sincerely urge you take your notebook, sit in a quite spot for 10 minutes and pen a few points down.

What is your self-Development plan? Subscribe to my U-Tube channel and watch the video on CANI. The link for the You Tube channel is: https://www.youtube.com/c/DavidNair a plan to continuously improve yourself. How? Sit think of the areas that you are passionate about. Areas that you feel would enhance your value as a person, areas that would contribute towards others development and at the same time leave you with a "feel good factor" List these down and go research on how you could enhance your value as a person. At the same time look at areas that could enhance your income generating skill. How could it be attained through a specialist workshop on that subject, read more on that subject or just listen and watch audio & videos on that subject. Work out a year plan broken up by month and week for such development and progress. Methodically work with it until you have stepped up to that skill set.

Vision, Purpose & Goals

Yes, we did address the mechanics of Goals, the process one would go through how to set goals. A recap the first thing you need to do, is to define your goals. This is very integral to your potential success as you cannot very well succeed until you know what it is that you want to achieve!

'Chase your dreams' people say. 'Follow your heart!' they announce.

But what if you do not know what your goals are? How can you go after the thing that will make you happy when you have no idea what that thing is?

"My 10 Minutes" 100 Goal Challenge

Stop here for a moment! before we proceed any further, I would sincerely urge you take your notebook, sit in a quite spot for 10 minutes and pen a few points down. I challenge you to write out 100 goals that you want to achieve in your life for yourself. For now, do not work with your family or your spouse. Once you have locked this in then you could reach out to them to help them. First start this exercise with you. Yes, I said it right 100. Go start it. Do not be disheartened if you only can clock up 10, 20, 40 or 50.

Many would not be able to go past 50 on their list. No issues. Start with that over time continue writing down the list and see when you can get to 100 and beyond. I had many who clocked up 200, 450 and 700 plus list of things they wanted to achieve before they die. The challenge is yours to start now.

In fact, one better I would suggest you purchase a separate book and call it Dream Book and set aside 10 pages in the front of that notebook for these lists. Start with the list now and keep adding to it, in time you will build a list bundle to work through your goals.

Have a Vision

I had touched about how vital it is for each of us to have a Purpose/Vision earlier in this book. As I have said a person without a purpose is like a ship, without a rudder. What happens to a ship without a rudder? It drifts and coast through the high seas allowing the waves, wind movements to push it in whichever directions it wants. This meandering is not in any way going to help that person achieve his/her goal. Why? Trying to work towards a goal without synchroneity is like trying to find a needle in a haystack...

That is why many find it so difficult to achieve their goals. Yes they go through the process, the steps all that but if the ambience, the inside environment/the outside environment and purpose are not in line... no matter how much you try, and try and try... it will never happen. Many will go through life not realizing why they are not achieving their goal, their happiness. They are where they are and painfully struggling to step up and have/live an empowered life, filled with true happiness.

Now, once the vision is missile locked, and a congruent goal is set in alignment with the purpose, then you work on the process internal/external alignment the process and step and guess what- it's inevitable that goal will manifest.

What is the Difference Vision & Goals?

A vision is a lot more abstract than a goal. A vision is not a plan or an idea but rather it is a lifestyle, a way of life, a state of affairs... a dream. Your goal will then fill in the steps from there...

To find your vision then, the simplest strategy is to try picturing your perfect life. Imagine you have been given a magic lamp and can make three wishes. Meanwhile, you also won the lottery.

What does this perfect life look like? What does it entail? Where do you see yourself? Who is there with you?

For some people, this vision is going to be the typical archetype of success. You might be as we described earlier, standing on top of a high-rise building, looking out over your domain, and wearing a smart suit.

But maybe that is not it. Maybe you are sitting in a hammock, drinking a cocktail while watching the sun set over a tropical ocean?

Or perhaps your dream is more modest? Maybe you imagine having a beautiful house, a beautiful wife/husband, and great kids. Maybe you envisage being able to spend all your time with those kids.

Or maybe, just maybe, your vision is completely bizarre to most people. Maybe your vision involves playing World of Warcraft all day. Maybe your vision is not even physically possible.

Do Not Let Others Define Your Goals

All of this is fine – and the first crucial lesson we need to learn here is that you must be honest with yourself. You need to be 100% brutally honest and if your dream is to enter a beauty pageant – as a guy – just admit it. Maybe your vision is just to be a bum and lie around the house!

Too many of us feel as though we must live the life that others set out for us. We feel as though we need to achieve what is considered the traditional view of success. We feel the urge to please our teachers, our parents.

And so, when someone asks us 'what is your goal?', we will often say 'to be a lawyer'.

We are too embarrassed to say that we just want to spend more time with our kids. And we're too embarrassed to say we want to be a pop star.

But what is the point of chasing someone else's dream? Go after the things that you feel passionate about and never feel ashamed of whatever they may be!

You Can Do Anything…Let Your Mind Loose Go Wild in Dream Building

From our earlier exercise of making our wish list, and from working in developing our Purpose and Vision we now come through in selecting our top five goals from that wish list, that we want to achieve this year. it is important that you do not hold back and that you write down the things you really want to achieve – no matter how farfetched or unimpressive they might seem to others.

We write these goals, utilizing the SMART approach described earlier.

If your goal – like the Dad from "Step Brothers" – is to become a dinosaur... then heck, write it down! Weird as it might sound.

The problem is, as we have already examined, too many of us have our sense of pride and even our identities tied up in 'what we do'. It is the first thing we need to unshield. Many are stuck with limiting beliefs that were implanted in us and it is so well entrenched that we are fearful of coming out of that pit.

But there is no reason it should be like this. Why not work simply to fund the lifestyle you really want and get your sense of accomplishment out of your achievements outside the office? How about using your free time in the evenings to write a novel? To compose a masterpiece. Or to set up a side business?

There is absolutely nothing stopping you, so get out there and go for it!

Want to be a rock musician? Fine – then all you need to do is to set up your own YouTube channel where you play your instrument. If you can build a big enough following, then you will enjoy a modicum of fame and some income from your music. You might even land a record deal! The same goes if you want to be a comedian, or an action star.

Want to be a writer? Just start writing! You can be anything you want to be – it is just success that is the hard part!

Want to have a mansion? Then create an epic budget and put all your savings into making that happen. You might have to build your own property but there is no reason this cannot be done if you buy the land – and it is more affordable than you probably think. There are ways you can get work done more cheaply too.

But you might not need a mansion to fulfil your vision. Maybe it is not the size of the home that matters but rather the décor. Maybe you would be just as happy with a large, modern and beautiful home with some stunning centrepieces.

And as it happens, this is highly achievable for less if you know how. A minimalist décor for instance means that you can spend less money on things you do not need and more on just a few stunning centrepiece items that will make your home truly memorable for instance.

And this is also how you are going to achieve that dream of becoming a dinosaur...

Because so often, it turns out that what we want is often not so simple. You might dream of being a dinosaur but ask yourself why you have this unusual aim. Is it because you want to be big and powerful? Do you want to be completely free? Do you love the natural habitats they live in? All these things are achievable and so you can be a dinosaur... in 'essence'. More likely, you might find that even though it is hard to become an astronaut, you could still indulge your love of space, the unknown and discovery by becoming an astronomer. Or maybe you could launch a camera into space as a hobby? Write a blog about space? Become an explorer?

To get to the bottom of what you want to achieve and to get to the 'essence', you can use a technique called "The Five Why's."

The Five Whys

The Five Whys is a series of questions that you ask yourself in order to get to the 'bottom' your own drive/motivations on pretty much any subject (and it also has a ton of other useful applications too). In this case, you're going to ask yourself 'why' you want to achieve a certain thing.

Why Do You Want to Be a Movie Star?

(Once you have written your answer, raise the next Why question on that response)

(Repeat this process five times – by which time you have drilled down to the heart of the matter and clarity of what it is that you really want to do will unfold. Try It out.

Why? Why? Why? Why? Why?

The first time you might answer that you want to be a movie star so that you can get a sense of accomplishment by sharing your work with everyone. The next 'why' you might answer by saying that you love performing and you love getting feedback from others. The next 'why' you might answer because you like to make others happy and so on.

And by getting to the essence of your goa will and your vision – the emotional hook that is motivating you – you will be much better at making yourself happy.

"My 10-Minute" The Five Why?

Sit back and jot down in the notebook, jot down your area of interest, the area that turns you on, when you think about it, your drive. Following that do ask yourself the series of questions that will further provide clarity and kick starting your vision. In time, working with this regularly, you will see it evolve into a vision that is going to bounce you out of bed daily, not just on a Friday.

Write Those Goals and Let Us Get Started

Now you know how to go about writing goals and having a vision, I want you to follow those steps and get a real picture in your mind of what you want to achieve and some steps on paper as to how you're going to get there.

Here is the thing though: you're going to write them down no matter how crazy they sound, no matter how off-the-wall they are.

Association Power

Working with Others

When it comes to being highly successful and going after the things you want in life, one of the most important factors that will have the biggest impact on the outcome, is just how well you work with others. And I am not just talking about your ability to get on with co-workers.

One thing that is important to recognize is that the decisions you make are not just decisions you will make for yourself. This is the part that is missing from a great number of different 'self-help' books. They tell you to go after whatever you want, and they tell you to be a go-getter... but what about, what your wife or husband wants? What about your children?

And what about the friends that you will miss when you're travelling the world without a care?

Likewise, how will your family take it when you decide that your dream is to become a high-flying CEO who is probably far too stressed and busy to spend the ideal amount of time with them anymore?

Unfortunately, our relationships in many ways prevent us from being entirely free and this is something you are going to have to navigate through if you want to be tremendously successful.

"My 10-Minute" List Your Top Five People You Most Associate With

Stop here for a moment! before we proceed any further, I would sincerely urge you take your notebook, sit in a quite spot for 10 minutes and pen a few points down. List down five people you most associate with. Why do you associate with each of them? What do you bring to the table in this association and what do they bring to the table in that association? Are they peer and above? What are you able to learn from them?

Ask for Forgiveness, Not Permission

As Tim Ferriss would say: ask for forgiveness, not permission. If you want to go on an incredible holiday of a lifetime with your friend, then you should go and not feel the need to ask anyone for permission. Take advantage of your freedom because otherwise you will only grow to resent the loved ones who you will grow to perceive as having prevented you from achieving the things you wanted to.

This does not mean that you should not be thoughtful and that you should make selfish decisions – it just means that you need to see your own hopes and dreams as being important and worth fighting for. And you should never apologize for them.

How do you balance both? One option is always to compromise. If you want to travel and your partner does not, then how about going on lots of small trips? If your partner fears you starting your own business, then do it on the side and agree to demonstrate that it can work before taking the plunge as we discussed earlier.

Or how about redesigning your goals and your plans to make sure there is a place for them in there? How can you turn this into something you will enjoy together?

At the end of the day though, there probably will always be some element of risk involved and if you are spending money then you are probably going to be putting your loved ones at risk in some cases too.

But in those cases, you just must acknowledge that you are taking this risk and shoulder the burden. Be willing to decide and stick with your convictions. If things go south, then be willing to pick up the pieces and take the blame. This is what it means to be an adult and it's what it means to take chances with conviction.

And it is when you are the most alive and the most courageous.

Being a Lion

Sometimes, going after your dreams is going to mean convincing your partner and getting them to get on board with your plans. Other times, it is going to mean challenging your boss or even going up against the establishment.

If your goal is to rise through the ranks of your current organization for example and if you want to be paid more for doing the job you're already doing, then you're going to need to stand up for yourself and make a case for a promotion.

This is something that many people will find terrifying and be completely loathed to do! Many of us prefer to live life without confrontation but again – life without confrontation is not really life at all.

Learn to be a little more aggressive in your life and to go after the things you want. Live like a lion and don't work quietly away hoping to be noticed. Again, ask yourself how well that has worked in the past?

Getting Feedback and Working with Others

People are not just obstacles to be overcome though. What you will also find is that they can be the tools to help you achieve the goals you want – and the partners to share your adventures with.

If you can get more people on board with your ideas, then you'll find that they suddenly gain much more momentum and they become self-sustaining even. Imagine working with your partner to create the trip of a lifetime or working with 5 friends to launch a business – imagine how much more you could accomplish.

And it's also important to spend some time listening to feedback and asking your friends and family what they think of your plans and dreams. This can be scary if you have staked a lot on your goals but any and all feedback is going to be very useful for helping you to avoid certain pitfalls – especially if you can seek out those with more experience than you.

Chapter Five

Take Ownership of your NOW

So, you are probably precisely aware of just how many times you have failed in the past. The brain is wired to remember negative experiences better. This is inherently built within the framework of our human evolution – from the cave men days. The predator/prey, victim/victor mindset. I will not go down that path in this book, but the long and short off this is, in whatever we do, we come from that negative approach , unless we condition mentally and consciously have a mental shift to come from the right required angle. It is not going to work any other way.

In addition, with the surge of online information, comments, product reviews etc, most people with positive experience do not think about it enough to post an online reviews. Inversely, most of the people who had a negative experience do think about posting an online review and in fact, many of them do. This gets re-emphasized into your brain and is anchors you on it. You will need to fight hard mentally to switch, otherwise you will go down the path that's not value add to you. The wiring of the brain, and the neuroplasticity can work for you or against you.

Your brain is wired to remember your failures better than your successes but that does not mean that you must let those past failures control you or even influence your actions in the present.

The Value of Your Mistakes and Learn from It

Of course, your mistakes do have some value. You can learn from your past mistakes and that is an advantage that we, as human beings have over most of the animals out there. We can learn from our failures; change the way we are doing certain things and then move forward with the new plan. If you try something and it does not work, then you can try something else later. So, do not hate your past mistakes. They have made you who you are today, which is obviously someone who is motivated and desires success, but do not dwell on your past mistakes too much either!

Do not live in the past. When you think about a past failure here are some of the ways that you may feel about it: embarrassed, depressed, frustrated, angry or fearful just to name a few. Now, throw all of those out the window when it comes to past failures. In fact, you are not allowed to be emotional about any past failure from here on out. You are going to look at the failure objectively, see what worked and what did not, and then move forward, because it is never as bad as you think it is.

My Credo – "You fail and fall seven times but get up eight times."

You Are Probably the Only One Who Remembers Your Failures

It is like that episode of Happy Days where Tom Hanks plays a man who went to high school with The Fonz, had some sort of problem with him, and spent a decade learning karate so that he could come back and whoop on Arthur Fonzerelli. You know what happened? The Fonz did not even remember him and was more than happy to apologize for past mistakes. The guy spent 10 years of his life dwelling on the past and the only reason that it grew from a tiny event to this huge persecution that he had to get revenge for was his own self-talk throughout those 10 years.

My Credo – "Drop your baggage and travel light."

Turning Potential Failures Into Successes

On the opposite end of the spectrum, another thing we do is to think negatively about future events as well. How is this connected to past mistakes? If your mind is dwelling on past mistakes, and your mindset is failure because of that, obviously, any future events will be seen through the same distorted lens. Many people let "what ifs" stand in their way. It's all in the way that things are worded and make no mistake; words are a very powerful thing. A comedian once said: 'I used to tell people I was trying to be funny and I couldn't get a gig to save my life, but then I told the next guy I was being funny, and he booked me!'

There are a lot of "what ifs" out there that could stop you dead in your tracks or spur you onto success depending upon how you word them. For example, instead of thinking that you are going to fail at something, and giving yourself that self-talk, take a positive spin on it and think that you are going to have massive success instead. Whenever you find yourself thinking a "what if" statement that is negative, stop yourself and turn it into a positive one. Eventually, this will become a habit and you will hardly ever find yourself having a negative thought like that again. What you will notice is that you start thinking "what if" positive statements and this will have a huge impact on your life; your attitude will improve, you'll be happier, and you'll be more willing to work on the things that will bring you success.

My Credo – "Turn your what "ifs" to I CAN"

Take It One Day at a Time – Phase One Me Time

Each morning when you get out of bed, work on your rituals. I would recommend that you work on these rituals daily. There are three Levels of these rituals that I practice and drive through my tribe for the last 3 decades. I would encourage you to take heed to its power and initially just do it on blind faith for 30 days. Then do an evaluation of the outcomes derived from it.

Phase One Rituals: 30 minutes is all I am asking of you – first thing in the morning – before you do anything else. This is the process you will go through. (I am talking coaching language here)

Step 1:

Go to the toilet, if necessary easy yourself, no brushing of teeth, or taking a shower. Get back to a quite location in your residence, where there is no disturbance, (Make this a permanent place that you use for this activity daily. Build this area up as your temple – the energy you exhibit here should be constantly empowering. I call this your Sanctuary. It could also be your daily reading spot and a spot where you will sit and ponder over your introspective exercises. Now sit in a comfortable position on the floor or a chair. Do this initially for 5 to 8 minutes. Do nothing but just sit still and feel your breathing. All I would like you to focus on is - your breathing, take deep breadths in, pushing your diaphragm down, as you do that your chest will push out, let it do that. Do not breadth pushing your chest out, we want you to push your diaphragm down and chest out. This will expand your lung capacity, which is what we want to happen. Get into the rhythm of doing this and continue to focus on your breathing. In through your nostrils out through your mouth. close your eyes and keep doing this for 8 to 10 mins.

Step 2:

Next phase 10 mins - you will do your incantation (an emotion pack affirmation with feeling at a peak state). You can do it in front of a mirror if there is one available, otherwise where you did your meditation would just as good, preferably (if you can) in a standing position.

Affirmation is a positive statement in the present tense, with the pronoun I.

As an example, I am Powerful. I am a positive thinking person. I am a winner, an endless of short powerpack empowering statements repeated like a mantra but with gusto and lots of emotion linked to it.

Make a list of 5 elements from when you did your self-evaluation. Write an empowering statement/affirmation using the three criteria mentioned above and this forms your affirmation. Repeat this for 10 mins.

Step 3:

From your wish list of things that you created, and want to achieve in life, select three of the items on the list and start visualizing them being achieved. "Image it in" and paint the picture of you enjoying the outcome manifested. As it had already been achieved. You from here walk, talk of its achievement.

Step 4:

Create a schedule for the day, think of something (productive/ empowering) that you can do to make yourself proud of what you have accomplished. Think of a reason that you should be proud of yourself and then do something to make that happen. For example, you have your entire Saturday to yourself. You can have a barbecue; you can watch some football on TV; you can work on the hobbies that you been neglecting, or you can spend eight hours working on your business. At the end of the day, which one of these do you think that you will be proud of yourself for?

This doesn't necessarily mean that you need to spend every waking minute that you're not at work or every bit of free time that you get working on your business, although you could, but it does mean that when you have the chance to work, don't procrastinate. Spending time on your project is not the only way to do something that you would be proud of either. If you put $100 in your savings account today, towards your online business in some way, you can be proud of yourself for that. Just do something every day to make yourself proud.

Summary Phase One of ME-TIME

Step 1: Meditation/Breathing Exercise 8 minutes

Step 2: Incantation/Affirmation 10 minutes

Step 3: Visualization 8 minutes

Step 4: Scheduling 4 minutes

Phase two and three of I-eXceL Wired For Success Me Time will be release in our second book YOUR WHY.

Do not Try to Do Too Much

One thing to keep in mind, however, is that you should limit what you are doing to a reasonable amount. Many people get excited about their goals and then they bite off more than they can chew and end up feeling like a failure. For example, you should spend no more than the eight hours discussed earlier on that Saturday where you find yourself with free time. You might think that you can work for 12 straight hours after a week of doing your job, and maybe you can, but it's more likely that you're going to burn out and then you'll feel as if you failed. Set goals that you can achieve, and you will be proud of yourself.

Decisions

**It's in moments of Decisions
That your destiny is shaped.**

- Tony Robbins

Start Making Better Decisions

With your Purpose well defined, your mission, your vision and your goals now more clearly mapped out, the next thing to do is to start following that blueprint to make your goals happen.

And this starts by recognizing what will support your goals and what is not helping you to get any closer to them. Too many of us work incredibly hard thinking that we are getting closer to our goals when we are just moving ourselves further and further away from them. We are just procrastinating...

Think About Every Decision

I hope that now you are starting to see everything fall into place and that you are starting to change your way of thinking.

Hopefully, you now recognize that you can get whatever you want from life as long as you know exactly what that is and you know how to set the most direct and most efficient course for getting there and making it happen.

It is time to start asking for the things you want, to stop apologizing and to start taking risks. These can be smart risks; they can be safe risks and you can be a lovely person while you go about it. But keeping your head down and hoping things fix themselves just will not cut it. It never has and it never will.

You need to start acting like a laser. That means having your mind fixed on what you want to accomplish and making sure that every decision you make is aligned with that goal.

Yes: every decision.

Why Every Decision Matters

We have already discussed how simply doing nothing is a decision and effectively means choosing never to progress or achieve the goals you want to achieve.

But the same goes for all those tiny decisions you make too, whether that means deciding what to wear today, or what to eat. You constantly have the choice to either bring your 'A game' and try to do your best, or to take the easier route and rest. If you really want to get to that end destination as quickly as possible, then you need to maintain the discipline and strength to do the former.

Likewise, though, it is also important to remember to take the time out to really enjoy where you have gotten too. Remember: success does not always mean pushing harder and further, it means creating the lifestyle that you have always wanted.

Just remember that all those decisions you took for granted as no-brainers: like deciding to take a promotion, or deciding to do the dishes yourself, have consequences. There is almost always more than one option.

Try to remember why you do the things you do. Always try to remember that dream and keep your vision in mind. When you do this, then you will have the means to go after what you really want from life and you will not be wasting your time anymore.

Misguided Strategies

But wait... didn't we say that you could make your goal anything? Didn't we say that it was okay to make your goal becoming a movie start? Or becoming a dinosaur? How are you going to make the decisions necessary to make those plans happen?

And what if you have responsibilities? Things you need to achieve. What if your kids are relying on you to pay their way through school – can you just drop everything and go travelling around the world?

Again, this comes down to mindset and I hope I am about to help you have a few 'eureka' moments here.

Firstly, recognize that fulfilling your dreams needs to take priority over most other things. That might sound selfish but think about what kind of father/mother your children would rather have: one who is exhausted and unfulfilled, or one who loves what they do and feels excited to go to work every day. What kind of example are you setting for them by spending your evenings in an office you hate, doing a job you hate, and still not having enough money to live comfortably?

The next thing to realize is that you can accomplish a lot of things much easier and more quickly once you stop thinking that your life should entirely revolve around your work.

Here is the irony – a lot of people will work incredibly hard and spend extra hours in the office just so that they can have more time with their family! They dream of being retired and they work so that their family can live comfortably.

If your goal involves spending more time with family, then this is absolute nonsense. All you are accomplishing is taking yourself further away from your family and providing for them less.

Your salary is not what dictates your wealth apart from anything else. You can get a raise of 2K a year by working incredibly hard and putting in extra hours, or you could rent the spare room out to students. Or you could sell trinkets on eBay. Or you could cancel that cable TV subscription and get slower Wi-Fi. You could stop paying for Netflix too.

What would you rather: pay for Netflix and more TV channels and take on hugely more stress at work, or just fix your budget and get more money that way while having more time to spend with family? You could move into a smaller house and pay less on your mortgage repayments, or you could sell your car and get a smaller, cheaper one.

A lot of people work incredibly hard because they want to 'save the money to go travelling'. Except, every time they get to that junction when they should just up and go, they realize that they are doing too well at work and that they cannot leave right now...

So, wouldn't it be better to change and get a job you can do online? Then you could travel while you earned money? Or how about taking a sabbatical from your current position? Or leaving work, only to find more work when you get back?

Why spend your youth working incredibly hard and making yourself ill with stress just to travel when you are too old to enjoy it? Why not just take long holidays now and live your life?

Why is working harder always the first answer that most of us think of?

The answer is that it is what we've been raised to believe by our schools and by the state. It is not their fault – it is the very central conceit of capitalism that you must work harder to get what you want. And we have been taught by others that working hard is the responsible thing to do for our families.

Too Bad They Are Wrong…

No matter what many people tell you, there is nothing inherently 'great' about wasting your life working at a factory, or at a company that sells staplers. You can work incredibly hard and feel like you are doing your job but at the end of the day, the world would keep ticking on even if you stopped. Meanwhile, your family and your dreams have been put on hold.

Often, the quickest way to achieve our goals is to take a pay cut, to move to a poorer part of the world. Often, we will find that we have enough money right now to build that dream house, travel the world or look after our families, if only we would focus a little less on work.

But we keep pushing harder and harder to 'succeed' in the traditional sense because we want to be seen to be successful and because that is what we've always been taught to do.

Even if your vision of success is the traditional one and you want to be that CEO, you're going to need to detach yourself from your current role in order to focus time and effort on your own business.

It is hard to break out of this mindset and this mentality but it is crucial if you're going to be successful.

The key here is to stop working blindly hoping things will get better and to instead ask what you want and what is really the best way to get it easily. And if that means spending less time at work and maybe raising a few eyebrows, then you must not be afraid of that!

Break Goals Into Bite Size Task or Activity -

Making Steps Out of Your Goals

> How do you eat an elephant?
> One bite at a time
>
> - Desmond Tutu

I have had many make comments to me, "I get overwhelmed with the amount of work that need to be done daily routine work and then these goals on top of it. What do I do? How do I cope?

So now you have a vision for what you want to accomplish, and you have embraced the things you really want from life, it is time to start making progress. And this is where you start creating goals and more specifically – steps – that you want to accomplish.

So, you want to get in shape eh? Get in line – so does the rest of the world, and most of them are still struggling to climb the stairs. And maybe it is that desire to 'get in shape', which is perilously vague and unhelpful, which is causing the problem.

The problem you see is that 'getting into shape' is not a goal. It is far too vague; it depends on your definition of 'shape' (round is a shape you know...) and it is not directly within your capabilities to control.

To be successful in any endeavor, you need to know how to correctly phrase what it is that you are trying to accomplish in your mind.

Why 'I Want to Get into Shape' Is Useless

Just saying you want to get into shape is so moot that I do not know where to start pointing out the problems. Of course, you want to get into better shape – everyone does. And if you make this your target then it's a target you can never accomplish (because you can always be in better shape) and never fail at (because you have an infinite amount of time to accomplish it). That's already incredibly disheartening, and when you try going to the gym and pushing yourself hard for a week only to notice your exact same shape as you were before and you're not really any closer to your goal... then you're quite likely to just give up.

So how should you have gone about creating this goal?

Where Do You Want to Be?

First, decide where it is that you want to be and what specifically you want to accomplish. The reason for this is that different health goals require different methodology – it is a different story burning fat compared to building muscle and it's no use lumping them together.

So, decide what would make you happy – increasing your biceps by an inch? Losing 1 stone? Note what your end goal is and write that down. But that is not your goal. This will come from the vision that you pictured earlier. What specifically does that vision entail and how can you go about writing a goal to get there?

The Steps (Inch By Inch is a Chinch)

Your next step is to write down exactly what it will take you to reach that destination. This will probably mean for instance going running three times a week for forty minutes. Or it might mean going to the gym to perform a split routine four times a week.

Now that is going to be your target – to repeat the crucial steps on that basis without fail for a certain amount of time. So, for instance your goal might be to 'go to the gym and lift weights four times a week for an hour without fail for the next three months'. Or it might be to 'eat no puddings for the next month'.

The time limit is on there simply to act as a light at the end of the tunnel – in other words to help you stay focused and dedicated and not get disheartened (so that you can say 'it's only a week left'). What is important though is that your goal is the process. That is because this is something that you can control directly, and this can give you much more of a sense of satisfaction while keeping you structured and focused. Now you are not even going to worry about how much weight you've lost or how much muscle you've built – because that will take care of itself.

The same goes for pretty much any other objective – Cranking down your goals this way will help master the task need to work through achieving those goals.

If you want to write a novel, do not aim to write a novel – aim to write two pages a night. If you want to travel the world, look at how much money you'd need to accomplish that and then aim to earn X amount every week to bring you closer and closer to that goal.

Work out your goals one step at a time and you will find this approach is much more effective overall.

Fear Setting

Even with these perfectly laid out steps though, you're going to find that it can often be hard to take the necessary leaps and become the thing you've always wanted to be, or to do the thing you've always wanted to do.

Why? Very often, the simple reason is fear – we are too afraid to take these massive leaps into the unknown and to take massive risks like quitting work, going part-time or putting ourselves on camera in front of the world.

It is understandable too – quitting your job will often mean losing your most important form of income – and likely you will have a lot of financial commitments that make that hard and scary. You probably have bills to pay, rent, a mortgage perhaps and you probably must look after your family and make sure that they get fed.

Maybe this is a particularly bad time – maybe you just got a promotion or maybe your wife is pregnant.

But here is the thing: there is never a good time to risk everything. If you are putting off starting a business because you are waiting for the right time, then it is never going to happen. If you are going to do it, then you need to just do it.

Of course, that is easier said than done though, so how do you go about overcoming the fear that has stopped you from going after your dreams? The fear that has kept you trapped.

One answer is something called 'fear setting'.

Essentially, the aim of fear setting is outlining your fears and to make sure that you recognize them for what they are. The idea comes from author Tim Ferriss, who wrote the book "The Four-Hour Workweek" and the nomenclature is intended to reflect the idea of 'goal setting'.

Until you write down your fears, they will remain abstract and intangible. And when they are in that format, they are impossible to overcome.

Write down your fears though and suddenly, you can take control of them and even find ways to combat them. Often, you will find that they are not nearly as serious as you made them out to be in your mind. This is remarkably like the idea of 'thought challenging' in cognitive behavioral therapy (CBT) and it can help you to take control over your thoughts in order to take control of your actions.

So, to take part in this exercise, I want you to take a minute to think about the vision and the goals and steps you formed for yourself. Maybe your plan is to start your own business selling cupcakes, great! In that case then, you might have decided that the best way to achieve the goals you have in mind, is to quit your current job, take out a bank loan and then use that loan to pay for an empty store and some marketing.

Wow, that is a massive risk and it probably threatens your current way of life in a big way. You will have a fear of 'failure' right now in your mind but at this point, that fear is again still abstract. So, let us fear set it. What are you afraid of? Some reasonable fears might be...

- Losing your job and never being able to achieve the same level of success again
- Being unable to pay off the loan, going bankrupt, losing your home and being unable to take our future mortgages
- Letting your family down, forcing them to live with less, perhaps driving your partner away
- Ending up homeless and destitute...
- Being a failure in front of everyone if it does not work out
- Being reckless by everyone even if it does work out
- Realizing that you do not like working here and that it is not as rewarding as you thought it would be

These all seem like pretty massive, insurmountable fears that perhaps are quite reasonable in many ways too. So, the plan is off right?

Wrong! Now that we have applied some fear setting, we can now go about deconstructing the things we're afraid of and seeing just how realistic those fears are. Perhaps we can even transform those lions into animatronics!

"My 10 Minutes" Two-step Process to Work on My Fear

Start by writing down how likely/unlikely each thing is to happen in reality:

- Losing your job and never being able to achieve the same level of success again – Not that likely, in almost every case, you'll find that you can pretty much walk back into the same job or an equivalent one. If not? Then you might have to work at a slightly lower level... but so what?
- Being unable to pay off the loan, going bankrupt, losing your home and being unable to take our future mortgages – This is somewhat possible, although it's highly unlikely you'd get to the point of completely bankruptcy or losing your home. You can get help from the government: you probably have savings, and you can sell off the property you bought to pay off most of the loan.

- Letting your family down, forcing them to live with less, perhaps driving your partner away – If your partner is supportive, then chances are they will want to see you go after your dreams. If they join in, it might even bring you closer.
- Ending up homeless and destitute... - This is almost completely impossible. Most countries and states have plenty of systems in place to make sure this does not happen. Homelessness is predominantly a problem for those who refuse help or who have drug problems. At the very least, you could stay on a friend's couch! You must have one who would not want to see you freeze...
- Being a failure in front of everyone if it does not work out – More likely, you will be a hero who took an amazing chance.
- Being reckless by everyone even if it does work out – Ditto. Except I would also like to point out at this point: who cares?
- Realizing that you don't actually like working here and that it is not as rewarding as you thought it would be – Always a possibility but seeing as it's obviously been playing on your mind this long, chances are that it is at least somewhat important to you and so you have to at least give it a go!

This is the equivalent of what is known in CBT as 'thought challenging'. The same technique can be used to overcome many different phobias, if you really believe the ratings that you are giving to each possibility.

This alone can help a great deal, but it is not enough. Next, I want you to go through your list one more time and come up with plans for how you are going to stop those bad things from happening. These are contingency plans that you can use to completely avoid the negative consequences of your plan going wrong. For example:

- Losing your job and never being able to achieve the same level of success again – Worst case scenario, you take up a menial job somewhere. It does not matter if it is enough to feed you and, in the meantime, you can work on plan B!
- Being unable to pay off the loan, going bankrupt, losing your home and being unable to take our future mortgages – Again, this is highly unlikely. But you can mitigate this scenario in numerous ways, by taking out insurance for your loan and business for example, or by selling the business off.

- Letting your family down, forcing them to live with less, perhaps driving your partner away – Discuss things thoroughly with your partner and then make sure you set aside enough money that they will be okay to live off.
- Ending up homeless and destitute... - Again, this is something you can avoid if you are to camp on a friend's couch.
- Being a failure in front of everyone if it does not work out – Simple: you try again, and this time prove them right!
- Being reckless by everyone even if it does work out – You explain yourself if it really matters that much to you!
- Realizing that you do not like working here and that it is not as rewarding as you thought it would be – You change the nature of the work. It's your business so you can run it however you like... make it more fun for yourself!

Mitigating Risk and Learning from Your Mistakes

Hopefully, by now, I have convinced you to be a little more risk taking and to change your mindset into one that involves going after the things you want in life. And hopefully, a side effect of that will be that you have started to accomplish more and see positive changes in your life.

But I am not recommending going blindly into everything here. I am not suggesting that you should always ignore the small amount of doubt you can hear in the back of your mind. Because sometimes, a little bit of doubt is a good thing. Sometimes, a risk is not worth taking.

It is important to be smart with this bullishness – not blind to the dangers! With that in mind, this part will be about balancing those two aspects...

We will star with the last part of fear setting...

Mitigating Risks

There is one more thing you are going to do while using the fear setting technique and that is to think about how you can avoid the risks altogether. This is an even better method than teaching yourself not to fear the worst-case scenarios because now you are removing those worst-case scenarios off the table altogether!

- Losing your job and never being able to achieve the same level of success again – This is a scary prospect so a good solution is to think about how you can make this project look like a great win on your CV. You could also speak with your current employer about the prospect of potentially coming back. You will often find they are happy to help out and to offer you a place when you get back!

- Being unable to pay off the loan, going bankrupt, losing your home and being unable to take our future mortgages – Okay then, how about you do not take out a conventional loan at all? Other options include getting a loan from family and friends, or even crowdfunding (which means raising money from the public via sites like Kickstarter). You could find an investor alternatively, or a business partner who has money to pour into it.

- Letting your family down, forcing them to live with less, perhaps driving your partner away – Remove this risk by using the above strategy and by discussing with your partner ways you can live on one salary. Another option might be to work a part time job, or how about earning some income online? You could even create more revenue models for this existing business, by selling your cupcakes online too, or by doing events.

- Ending up homeless and destitute... - Again, the above strategies will ensure this isn't a risk.

- Being a failure in front of everyone if it does not work out – If you are that worried, you don't have to tell everyone. Or how about opening this more as a side project or hobby and explaining you're not in it to make money.

- Being reckless by everyone even if it does work out – If you are worried this is reckless then you could create a multi-stage plan to launch your business. Before opening the store, you could start out by doing events or selling at fairs. This is something you could do at the weekends and then you could gradually reduce the amount of time you are working in the office.

- Realizing that you do not actually like working here and that it is not as rewarding as you thought it would be – The above solution will address this problem too.

By going through this process, you now have a much safer and more resilient business model and hopefully you are less afraid to take the leap. And once again, I hope this has demonstrated to you that you do not have to wait. You do not have to wait to earn enough money to finally have the time to quit your job and launch your cupcake shop – in fact, using that method will ensure it never happens. You have the means to make it happen right now, with crowdfunding, by making a smaller business first and bootstrapping, or how about using PayPal?

This same logic can be applied to any number of different situations and goals too. For example, many people will stay stuck in a job they don't like and they'll tell people that they can't leave because their family is relying on their income.

This is sounding very much like they intend to leave their job and then look for a new one. In which case, yeah... that would be reckless! But instead, the much, much smarter option would be to find the job you want to do in the evenings after work and only leave it when you are happy with that job.

Oh and this is also how you set up your own online business – work a few hours in the evenings, earn some money that way and then quit your job when you're reliably making enough to live off of!

Recognize the Power of Your Choices

The thing to recognize is that every tiny choice you make is really a decision. You might think that you are trapped and without the ability to make choices. You may feel as though your life has been thrust on you and that you have just been a hapless victim. But as I said before: you chose to be here. And if you felt as though you never got the choice, then chances are that it was your inaction that kept you here. That is still a choice though – choosing to do nothing is still a choice!

And with this in mind, it becomes incredibly important to think hard about your choices going forward and to be able to look back at those decisions you made in order to know how to change things for the better. What decisions have worked for you and which have not?

The first place is probably to start with that decision to take no action. The decision to let fear and social pressure push you into a job that you do not enjoy. How did that decision turn out for you?

Now let us extrapolate that for a moment and imagine that you continue making that same decision for many more years to come. How will your life look if you keep on making the same decisions? In this case the reality is probably much scarier than any of the possible futures we looked at when fear setting.

If you continue with your inaction, then you are going to end up working the same job probably for the rest of your life. Your lack of physical activity in the evenings (owing to your lack of movement during the day), will lead to your body gradually deteriorating as you gain weight and collect aches and pains. You will never live your dreams of running a business, being a rock star or whatever else it was you wanted to achieve. And you will continue to be completely unrewarded in what you do. Every day will continue to be one slog after another and one day you will wake up and be 80.

That is the price of the decision to do nothing.

Look at this decision, weight it up and then decide if you can continue to live that way. Hopefully, this will help you to recognize the importance of all those decisions.

And that also includes the decision you make to not work on your business tonight, to not workout tonight...

Kaizen or CANI (Continuous and Never-Ending Improvement)

This might sound like a lot and it might sound daunting but that is why it can pay to keep in mind the principle of Kaizen. Kaizen means making small, incremental changes that all add up into something big and profound.

So that is one mistake you should look back on and learn from. What others are there?

Well, perhaps you can remember examples of when you tried to make changes in your life in the past and it did not work out. What caused those failures?

For these changes to come forth, a brief on what are your developmental plans. If you want to progress you will need to change. Staying where you are and hoping to get a different result is called insanity. Hence, simply put, create a developmental plan for what you need to do to improve yourself. – based on the goals of where you are and what you want to get out of Life, the things that you always dreamt of and what you wanted to achieve.

What additional skills you will need?

What books would you need to read?

What course/programs that you will need to attend?

What U tube you need to watch and learn from?

What podcast are you listening to step up your standard?

Chapter Six

Clarity is Power

**Clarity of Body, Mind & Spirit is the
Kick start to a Congruent Life**

- davidnair

What Does Congruency Have to Do with Life One Would Ask....

To live a congruent life simply means to be living in space that you have consciously created for yourself. A space that serves a great purpose and acts as the foundation upon which you will manifest excellence into your life. This is a space where you have taken delicate care to tend to, always making sure it is neat and tidy and ever-expanding.

If you are sitting there asking yourself if you even have such a space, do not worry you are not alone. In fact, most of us do not consciously take the time to give ourselves one moment of relaxation at the end of a full day. Somewhere along the line, it is as if a new software was installed in our psyches that told us life always had to be hard; and that if it wasn't, then we were doing something wrong.

The Process Plant Approach to Life

Many have a process plant approach to life. A life that they have "cut, copy & pasted" from their parents, relatives, and generation prior. Please do not misunderstand me. Its fine to do so, but evaluate that journey of your life...

Born, go through kindergarten, primary, secondary, tertiary schools, come out of college or university and work for four if not five companies, retire and what next? Waiting to be buried?

We need to look at this wholistic life balancing the four quadrants of Career/Business, Family, Recreation & Social and spiritual (not necessary religion). At I-eXceL Wired For Success, we will introduce you to these concepts and take you into the developmental phases at subsequent session in generating a wholistic balanced blueprint of life.

Have this *"empowering, progressive life blueprint"*, rather than *"meander through life blueprint"*, on a process plant regime and at the end wonder where has life gone? Is this all that I had worked for? What has happened, life just fly past me.

If your WHY is Big enough, the HOW does not matter.

- davidnair

To kick start this whole process let me point out that there has never been a good time to sit down and think about what you want to accomplish in life. What is your purpose of being here? What and where do you want to be in five years, ten years and so forth from now. We understand that everyone is busy.

Our next book titled Your Why? At our follow up live sessions we will teach you how to define your WHY? This is despite many of us having a busy life, we are drifting without that Definite Major Purpose. We will walk you through that process and when you come out of that washing machine cycle, you will see with clarity what, how, when to do certain things thereby and see the outcome with clarity.

Now, to commence part of that journey, please sit in a comfortable chair by the table with a pen and pad. Put aside 30 minutes, turn of mobile phone, TV, and no interruptions. This would make a world of difference in your life....

And it is not that hard. You probably already have a good idea of what you want to do, but you may not have it written down. Or maybe you have done this exercise before, but you have not updated your goals for a while. Now's the time to do it. Invest in a notebook – A journal that we call Your Dream Book.

Five Steps to Scale Up with Your Clarity Dream Book

1. *Where and How do I startt?*

    What would your epitaph be? Think when you leave this world what would you like people – your family, friends, work colleague, acquaintance strangers, to say about you at your funeral. This comes from Stephen Covey's 7 Habits of Highly Effective People — the habit called "Begin with the end in mind." It is also highly effective. Imagine you are at the end of your life, looking back. What would you like to have accomplished? What kind of person would you like to have been?

The interesting note about this is, start living your life so that you will eventually get to that point.

2. **What are some ideas for life goals** you would like to achieve before you die? Jot down whatever comes to your mind. Do not question? Do not analyze? Do not stop information and ideas flow? Now is not the time on moment to analyze. We constantly are in the analysis mode, we analyze, reanalyze until we get exhausted with analysis. Do not get paralyzed with analysis.

The goals can be in many areas, but here are a few to start with: professional, education, family, spiritual, travel, recreation, hobbies, community, charity. You can probably think of more, and you don't need to have goals in all these areas. Just a few topics to get you started.

3. **Keep working and play with the list. Refine your list or expand it.** After the initial brainstorm, you may want to fine tune on the goals into the four quadrants of Career/Business, Family, Recreation & Social and spiritual (not necessary religion), Consciously work on it trimming it down and expanding on the base goals. Discipline on working with this at least once a week. Make it fun, and in time have the family involved in it and you will see the difference in how the family begins to bond together. We will be covering this in greater detail in our workshop session. Pays to Dream Big. You will see how this have huge impact on once wellbeing and the balance of specifics chemicals within our body, because we are riding the way of the happiness factor. More to come on it.

4. **From that list break it down into a timeline chart. 10 yrs.,**

What should you accomplish in the next 10 years **5 years 3 years 1 year and 6 months and 3 months and monthly** for each of these goals? Once this is mapped out in such a timeline, you would be surprised how clear your thinking would become. Because of this clarity, how much more relived a person you end up being.

5. **I refer to this step as "Follow Niki" - It is time to act!** I like to take my monthly goals and make a to-do list for this week. What can I do today to further my goals? And if I can get just one thing contributing towards that goal, I am done for that day. I've done a lot to make those dreams a reality!

Take a step towards your dreams today by writing them down and planning.

So, are you ready to make some goals? To discuss goals, we are going to use the analogy of a vacation that you are traveling to by car. The goals that you set are like the ultimate destination, the place that you are going to. The vehicle that you are going to use to get there; are the short-term goals that you'll be achieving along the way but without a very specific ultimate destination, you aren't going to get anywhere. That is like trying to drive to Florida on your vacation and saying that it is somewhere "over there" east of you.

What Are Specific Goals?

What exactly are specific goals? Let us take one of the goals that you probably have, because everyone trying to achieve success has this goal; to make more money. Your goal cannot just be the goal of making more money, becoming rich or financial independent either, because those things mean nothing specifically. So, how are you going to know when you get there? How will you know if you are on the path to get there? Unless you make your goals specific, you will have no direction; no specific place on the map that you can arrive to and know that you are in the right place.

So, let us take the example of wanting to make money. Instead of having a goal that is so general, try creating a goal with something like: increase income by $10,000 per year by the end of the year, or by the 12th month; if you happen to be in the middle of the year. So, you'll know if you've achieved that goal, because now you can investigate your bank account, or at your balance sheet, and see if you have earned that extra $10,000 in the past 12 months or not. Also, when you get to month six, you'll be able to look and see just how much on track you are! If you are around halfway there, you know that you're on track. But if you haven't made anything yet, you really need to step up during the next six months.

Aim High, Like the Air Force

Do you know what you are capable of? You might think you do, but for most people what they can achieve is quite different than what they think they can achieve. You have probably heard the axiom: whether you think you can, or you cannot, you are right. People have set world records in athletic events, and experts have deemed some of them the fastest or best the human body is capable of, and then someone from a remote part of the world didn't get the memo that there was a limit as to what the human body was capable of until after they'd already broken the record.

Set your goals higher than you think you can achieve. Of course, do not set them outrageously high to the point where they are unrealistic, but set them higher than you think you're probably capable of. For example, our previous goal of earning an extra $10,000 in 12 months is reasonable and probably achievable depending on what you do to make it happen. If your goal is to make $100,000 over the next 12 months, that is unrealistic. But what if your goal were to make an extra $15,000 in 12 months? You might think that you are only capable of making an extra $10,000 but by setting the go higher you have something to aim for, and suppose you only make $12,000; that is still $2000 more than your original goal.

Putting Goals into Action

You want to make a list of around five goals to start with. The number is not important; it is arbitrary. What is important is that you create enough goals that will allow you to accomplish something substantial in the next 12 months, or five years, or whatever your timeframe is, and not so many goals that you have no chance of achieving them all. Then, for each goal, you are going to plan of action. Earlier we used the analogy of driving a car to a vacation destination. Your plan of action is that car; it is the vehicle that is going to take you all the way to the end where your success waits.

Your plan of action is going to take you from where you are now all the way to the result, which is your goal. It is going to include milestones, or places that you stop along the way to check your progress as well as specific small goals that you will need to achieve to get to the big goal. It is sort of like playing a videogame – you must beat all the easy monsters before you get to the big boss at the end of the level. If your goal is to make an extra $10,000 in the next 12 months, then you need to know what specific things you need to do to make that happen. Are you planning to start an online store? Are you making investments? Whatever your method is, you will have specific things that you need to accomplish, and that makes up the framework for your plan of action.

What If You Do Not Know How to Get There?

Sure, you might be saying, this is all well and good, but what you do if you do not know how to get to your destination – or achieve your goal. There are several ways that you can figure it out. You can do research online, you could write to some of the people that you admire and that you know of had success and asked them how they were able to achieve their goals. You can read a few books or get advice from family or friends. There are many things that you can do to learn how to get from point A to point B.

Chapter Seven

Are You Giving Your Best?

**Whether you think you can or think you can't
You are right!**

- Henry Ford

Have you ever had a job that you did not like? When you woke up in the morning, you had to drag yourself out of the bed and force yourself to go to your work. This might be the job that you are working right now. Well, you know how when you get to work, sit down in your cubicle, and begin crunching those numbers your heart really is not into. You are just not giving your best self to your employer. At most, you're giving about half of it, and while this might get you a pay check every month, you're not doing what you love!

So instead, you should give yourself – your best self – which is the person that is going to work the hardest, the person that is going to persevere the longest and the person that is going to ultimately take you to success. You want to be the kind of person that other people will look at and comment on how hard you work and how much you give to your business. Every single day you need to be the best self that you can. That does not mean that you need to be perfect. No one is perfect. But it does mean that you can look back at the end of the day and say: "I did a good job today."

Basics That You Can Do as a Person to Be Your Best Self

- Do not show up late for work, business, or an appointment – online or offline. Show up early instead. Yes, sitting down at your computer to do whatever it is that you need to do to make your business work, whether that is marketing, building a website or simply finding a good opportunity for entrepreneurial success; that is going to be your job. You should be twice is committed as you are to your day job to the time that you spend working on your business and building your success.

- Be willing to help others. If you encounter someone that could use some of the skills that you possess, consider spending some of your free time helping them. For example, if you're a graphic designer, and a colleague needs a business card, although you don't directly benefit from creating a business card for your friend, it could pay back dividends down the road. If there is such thing as karma, you will be building the good kind as well.

- Develop relationships. No one succeeds in a vacuum and the relationships that you build with other people can help you much later in life as well as build lasting friendships. Some people will only build a relationship with someone who they think is in a position to help them with their business and this is a huge mistake because you never know what might happen in the future and when somebody that you have developed a friendship or working relationship with suddenly finds themselves in a position to help you achieve success and is willing to do so.

- Start to cultivate patience. Many entrepreneurs want success right away. There is nothing wrong with this, but you are probably going to want to learn to be patient if you're in business for yourself because it can take a while to see the fruits of your labour. Rarely is someone an "overnight success." It is much more likely that they worked hard to get where they are, and you just were not aware of it.

- Become flexible when you must be. One of the problems that entrepreneurs run into, particularly if they are the type of personality that likes a very rigid set of rules and working guidelines, is getting stuck at an impasse because something happened that they couldn't plan for. Things are going to happen with your plan for success, no matter how much you try to prepare for every eventuality and the only way that you are going to overcome those challenges is to be flexible.

- Be honest; use integrity and all your personal and business dealings. If you think that a product that you are considering is of poor quality, or there is some reason why it is not a good product to sell, do not sell it. If someone comes to you and offers to make your website rank a whole lot higher using black hat SEO techniques, tell them no. You want to be the kind of businessman (or woman) that customers can depend on and trust and violating that trust will cost you.

Do Not Multitask

Everyone talks about multitasking like it's the greatest thing since the Macarena, but the truth is multitasking can cost you time spent on your project. In fact, studies show that you not only have a 40% reduction in the amount of work that you get done, but that you might be damaging your brain by multitasking. Instead of multitasking, give whatever project that you are currently working on your full focus. In fact, give your current project 110% and watch your productivity rise drastically. People tend to like multitasking, either because it offers them variety and makes work seem to go by faster or because they've been told it increases their productivity.

Make Sure Your Heart is in It

You want to make sure that your heart is in what you are doing on two different fronts. First, make sure that you are passionate about what you are doing to achieve success in your completely invested in the project. But also, make sure that you are invested in whatever specific project that you are currently working on. If your heart is not in it, then consider outsourcing it to someone who is more passionate about it than you are. For example, if writing is not your forte, hire a freelancer. If you have been trying to design a company logo and you find yourself getting frustrated, consider hiring a graphic designer or using one of the premium logo services online.

Mindset of Excellence, Mindset of Persistence

This is best described by the following story of the French Spiderman Alain Robert who finally managed to climb the 88 stories off the tallest building in Malaysia, Petronas Towers. It was his third attempt, after two failed trails, one in 1997 and the second in 2007.

He never gave up following each time that he failed Alain went back to the drawing boards – the fundamental that one had to do to scale a building. He practiced, and practiced, and practiced, and practiced, finally he attempted for the third time. Walla, he made it – Was its chance, or choice? He is quoted as saying, "With due respects to Malaysia, I came to finish something, despite what the press put up, despite what was mooted in the climbing circles." He was focused, he was on a mission, he persisted until. "Climbing the Petronas all the way to the top is one of my dreams." He described himself as determined but also "a little bit stubborn."

Fascinating guy, I wonder what went on in his mind, as he makes his climb, "I hope I do not slip" – a rhetorical question. Did he have the doubt fling past him, yes numerous times and its normal. If it did not, then there is something wrong. It normal for the "Doubting Thomas's" to take up space in your mind. What is not normal is what do you do when it takes space in your mind? How do you handle this situation, whilst it is there occupying the space? These are all are shifts in habit, rituals that will only come into play if practiced. it just does not happen. It needs to be worked on, it needs to continuously be practiced on, not till it is perfect, instead till it becomes second nature.

As an illustration let me ask you a simple question? What is 6 multiplied by 2? You will respond 12. What is 4 multiplied by 4 and your answer is 16, what is 7 multiplied by 7 and you will answer 49. Now, today you can vomit this answer without evening thinking. Am I right? You so confidentially spit the answer out. Now just rewind the tape to when you were in primary school at the arithmetic class of multiplication table. You were asked the question 6 multiplied by 2, 4 multiplied by 4 and 7 multiplied by 7 and in each instance you will look at the teacher in bewilderment, sometime embarrassed, sometimes, scratching yourself, sometimes wondering why were you there? Then the teacher, comes towards you and gives a slight whack on your bottom with a scale, and she give you the answer – 12 or 16 or 49. Following which you will recite after her the multiplication table. And over time you master it, to such an extent that now without thinking you can just recite or call out the right answer.

There was Pain for Gain to happen. Action for reaction, cause, and effect. The laws of the universe say so. Similar with shifts in habits or rituals the same pattern for mastery is required, we cannot wing it, we n need to persist with our practices of mastering effective habits until it becomes second nature. Many do not have the patience, many do not have the tolerance, many do not have the commitment. I ask of you Are you really wanting that change to happen. Then no questions, no comprise, no halfway attempts. Just practice, practice, and practice, until mastery is attained.

Most would ask, "what have I learnt from Alain Roberts?" As opposed to reflecting and asking, "what can I learn from Alain Roberts?" The need and what to learn, to improve should be well grounded within us, such that it's never ending, and perpetually till the day we die. As I had previously said in my earlier story, this thirst, this hunger for growth will stop the day we die.

That is what we drive in our programs – creating that mindset for perpetual development in search for Excellence.

In my 20 yrs. working with 50 of the top company's in India, putting through 50000 + participants, (direct connects) through various development programs, I found individuals are extremely knowledgeable in their domain of expertise. Take them out of that pond and immerse them in the ocean, they would be lost, as their fundaments for life skills are limited. They are a big fish in a small pond. I would rather be a small fish in a big pond, constantly sharpening my skills to be at the cutting edge and hence perform at that level. Imagine at what level will the outcome be pitched.

This circle of excellence is an amazingly simple four step process. Many do not realize how simple things, impact our body, mind, and spirit. This "temple" of ours, as I commonly refer to it is there for us to excel and give back what was so graciously given to us by the universe, for some, by god for other.

Circle of Excellence

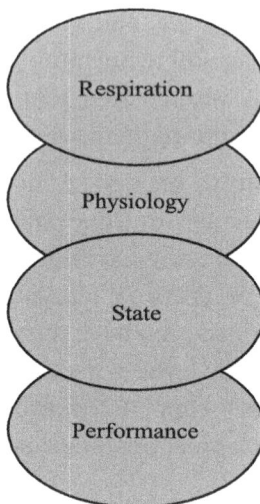

What is the most precious gift given to us? Take a few moments STOP, reflect, think hard and what is your answer?

How many would have answered, it is my breath, the gift of my breath of life. STOP again, take a deep breath, and let it out another deep breadth and let it out. It is that fundamental breadth that triggers everything in us. Without it we will not be here. The moment we are born, the doctor wacked our bum to give us that initial kick start to breathing.

Ever watched the birth of a giraffe? Mother giraffe will be standing to give birth, the baby drops some three to five feet depending on the height of the mother giraffe. The mother giraffe watches if the baby is moving and if its does not, the mother giraffe, gives the baby giraffe a hind foot kick. One that hurls the baby some ten to fifteen feet. The mother watches if the baby giraffe moves and if it does not move the mother giraffe gives it another kick. Eventually the baby giraffe, if not still born, begins to breath and stands on its weak legs. the baby giraffe starts its journey of life.

That breath of life stays with us till our last moment on earth. After that first catalyst to help us breath, has anyone been taught or trained how to breath? In most cases the answer is no. Note it is the most important, instead vital to truly learn how to breath. Why as its this activity that generates all our performance. It is unfortunate we cannot go to a school to learn to breath, except the few who have commenced yoga, meditation and had some lesson in breathing through Pranayama. Our master classes we will be covering this aspect from the angle of understand how best to maximize out on our performance.

Physiology

What is Physiology?

Have you ever felt miserable or depressed? At the time did you pay attention to your body? How was it moving? How was it positioned? What were your eyes focusing on? What kind of gestures did you make? How were you breathing? What sort of facial expressions did you make? Were you even conscious of these signals? Or did you simply not care to give it any attention?

If you paid little to no attention to your physiology at the time, then you clearly missed out on an incredible opportunity to unlock the creation process of your emotional experience.

Your state-of-mind is intrinsically connected to your physiology. In fact, the two are so closely intertwined that slight changes in one can lead to significant changes in the other.

Physiology is a broad term that refers to:

- Movement of the body
- Gestures made
- Posture
- Eye-gaze or focus
- Rate and depth of breathing
- Level of muscle tension
- Facial expressions
- Position of limbs
- Alignment of spine and head

The Mind-Body Connection

The mind reflects your physiology by responding to its levels of tension, the rate of breathing, the speed of movement, and to your attention and mental focus. Likewise, your body mirrors your thoughts, feelings, mood, and responds to your state of mind, the questions you ask and the words you speak daily. Both are intrinsically connected and intertwined in an intimate dance that lasts a lifetime.

What Does All This Mean?

If the mind and body are intrinsically connected — meaning that one has a direct effect on the other — then it poses the argument that if we directly and consciously take control of one, that it will directly influence and transform the other. Therefore, by taking the time to purposefully adjust how you use your body will immediately influence your state of mind and could likewise dramatically transform the course of your decisions and actions.

The Physiological Experiment

To prove how powerful this can be, follow along and participate in the following physiological experiment.

In a moment I will ask you to experiment by adopting two states that are on opposite sides of the emotional spectrum. The first state is depression, and the second state are confidence.

Take time now to experience each of these states separately by adjusting your physiology accordingly with the following guidelines. Please be sure to spend at least 2 minutes experiencing each emotional state exactly as described.

Experiencing a State of Depression

Think about your problems and mistakes.

Speak slowly, methodically and in a monotone voice. Walk rigidly and slowly while shuffling your feet.

Make sure you slouch your shoulders, sink down in your posture, and feel the tension building up in your body.

Breathe in a shallow, uneven manner using your upper chest.

Make sure that your eyes are looking down and have a very narrow range of focus.

Wear a disheartening frown on your face. ☹

Before switching to the next emotional state, shake your body out from head to toe for 10 seconds.

Experiencing a State of Confidence

Think optimistically about solutions and positive outcomes. Speak passionately with increased volume and tempo.

Walk quickly with purpose ensuring that your back and shoulders are straight and that you are moving your body freely.

Make sure to use gentle gestures and walk lightly on your feet. Breathe using your abdomen evenly and deeply.

Make sure your eyes are looking forward and that you are using your peripheral vision.

Wear a cheeky grin on your face. ☺

Now that you have experimented with both states, what is your verdict? How did each emotional state feel? Was there a distinct difference between the two states? What role did your body play in helping you transform your state of mind?

If you completed the experiment correctly you probably realized how small changes to your physiology can dramatically transform your state of mind. We make these shifts and changes all the time without even thinking about them. Maybe from this moment onward we can do them proactively, consciously and with purpose.

"My 10 Minutes" Confidence

This whole segment is best understood through practice. Experiential learning. So please participant in the exercises. Ensure your notebook is by your side. Once done the first time you might in some case what to repeat it daily for at least thirty day to master the practice. Excellence is a habit.

Experimenting with Your Physiology

Find Your Peak State

The most successful people in the world, whether in business, sports or any other career path are at their best when they are working from within their optimal peak state. This state means different things to different people. It's therefore important to identify the peak state that is right for you — allowing you to work to your highest potential at any one moment in time.

Here are some guidelines that will help you find your peak state:

Cultivate Awareness

Start by becoming aware of your thoughts, emotions, and current frame-of-mind. Also, pay attention to your mental focus and how you perceive things and circumstances. This awareness will help you gain deep insights into your current state of mind while assisting you with your search for your peak optimal state.

"My 10 Minute" Physical Body Awareness

Extend Awareness to Physical Body

Now, begin extending your awareness to your physical body. Ask yourself:

How does my body feel?

How am I sitting or standing?

What is my body doing?

This awareness will help you manage your body more effectively as you strive to maintain an optimal state of mind.

Cultivate Empowering Traits

There are certain traits and characteristics that are naturally conducive to bringing forth an optimal state of mind. For instance, by taking time to cultivate charisma, passion, enthusiasm, curiosity, optimism, patience, and persistence will instantly help empower your thoughts and transform how you use your body daily.

"My 10 Minutes" On State Cultivation

To begin cultivating each of these states simply ask yourself:

How would I use my body if I were filled with passion or enthusiasm?

How would I use my body if I were curious and fascinated about my problems?

How would I use my body if I had an incredible amount of patience? How would I use my body if I were the most charismatic person alive? What would I say to myself?

What would I focus on?

How would I focus on things?

What gestures would I make?

How would I breathe?

What would I think about?

How would I walk?

How would I talk?

How would I interact with others?

What kinds of decisions would I make?

What kinds of actions would I take?

How would I look?

Focus on the Positives

It is easy for us to get completely absorbed in our day-to-day problems. In such instances, we tend to focus on what is not working or on what is difficult. This often leads to limiting emotions and likewise physiological changes.

To experience our peak optimal state, we need to always focus on solutions and opportunities that will naturally encourage us to keep moving forward towards our goals and objectives.

"My 10 Minutes" On Focus on the Positives

Keep a record for a week write down every time your mind heads off to what is not working or what is difficult to do. On the weekend put some time aside to find solutions for what is not working an what is difficult to do and why? As a peer, friend or your coach, mentor, mastermind, or support group, for solution that you are having difficulty to find.

Model Successful People

In addition to everything we have discussed thus far, it is also prudent to model the peak states of successful individuals whom you admire. These people are successful because of the states that they can maintain consistently over time that help them perform at the highest levels.

"My 10 Minutes" On Modelling Successful People

Make a list of successful people you admire. Make a list of what their peak states that you have observed.

Study these people, model their states, and soon you too will begin replicating their results.

"My 10 Minutes" How to Find Your Peak State

Sit down and go through go what has been covered above to achieve Peak State. The first time around it could take 30 mins. Spend the time to go through it. After the first attempt repeat this exercise for 30 days for mastery. Always remember excellence is a habit.

Writing Out Your Physiological Recipe

In the previous section, we identified several empowering traits that are critical for success in any field of endeavour. We will now look at traits that you personally believe are absolutely critical to your success in your area of expertise. Let us unlock your physiological recipe.

Step 1: Select Critical Trait

Select a trait that is required to achieve your goals and objectives. It could, for instance, be confidence, creativity, enthusiasm, passion, or motivation. Choose just one empowering state that will have the greatest lasting positive impact on your life.

Step 2: Identify Time You Experienced State

Think back to a time when you experienced this state. Reflect on this experience and identify how you used your body and gestures, where and how you focused on things, how you breathed, what you said to yourself, etc.

Go through all the reference points we discussed in the previous section and identify in detail on paper the exact psychological and physiological recipe you used to get into this state-of-mind.

Also take time to consider what events, people or circumstances might have triggered this state and how you responded at the time.

Step 3: Adjust Your Physiology

As you think about this peak optimal state, begin shifting your physiology to match your experience. While you are doing this, ask yourself:

What am I thinking about? What am I focusing on?

How am I focusing on things?

How does this affect or change my physiology?

Make a mental note how your body is responding to this emotional state. This will help you unlock your physiological recipe.

Step 4: Practice and Anchor State

Once you have unlocked your physiological recipe, now comes time to lock it away for good in the recesses of your mind. To do this, you must ensure that you form a new habit that is lasting and transforming. This is best achieved by creating an anchor that involves physically anchoring the desired state to a part of your body.

As you think about this optimal state and adjust your body, accordingly, lightly tug on your earlobe when you feel you are at the peak of your emotional experience. Do this several times per day over a period of a few days. If done correctly, you will establish a lasting anchor that you can use at any time to call forth your optimal state and physiology.

Read more about creating powerful anchors here, here, and here.

Developing Peak State and Empowering Physiology

Many are unaware of how we go through the process of developing such peak state to empower our physiology.

Rapidly Shifting Your Physiological State

When we feel disheartened and miserable it is easy to fall prey to our emotions and exceedingly difficult to find the motivation to change our physiology and movement. However, if we want to maintain the highest levels of productivity, then we must as often as possible maintain a peak emotional state.

"My 10 Minutes" How to Dig Oneself Out of a Lazy Slump?

Here are some quick and easy ideas that will get your body moving and help you dig yourself out of a lazy slump:

Listen to energizing or inspirational music.

Start dancing and moving your body to music.

Hit a punching bag.

Do some exercise.

Go for a walk.

Take a warm bath or shower.

Sit still and breathe deeply through your abdomen.

Each of these suggestions will help you shift your physiology and improve your focus and concentration. As a result, you will become more active and productive throughout the day.

Alert Attention:

Study of State in Depth for the Few Who Love This Subject

Why do we emphasize state and state management so much? The quick answer is that your state determines which inner resources you have access to.

The only thing standing between your present state of wanting something you do not have and your desired state, which is having what you want, is access to a resource or resources. I refer to it as the Gap

I once heard Tony Robbins say that the greatest resource is resourcefulness. While I agree it is hard to put that into practice so let us break it down.

You can divide up your life into different contexts like personal life, professional life, school life, social life, etc. Choose one context and think about what resources do you need to access to be your best in that context.

For example, in your work life you might need focus, determination, and creativity.

Then ask yourself what state do you need to be in to access those resources? Perhaps the best state is one where you are relaxed and yet engaged and intentional. We can call the state "Workflow" state.

You do not have to start with resources. You can start with the state by remembering a time in the context you have chosen when you were performing at your best. Step into it or associate into the memory and access the state. Name the state so it is easier to recall it later when you want to and notice what relevant resources you are accessing and name those as well.

You may want to be in a state where you have access to all your resources all at once, all the time. While that may be possible (but unlikely), the state would be so general it would be hard for you to focus on any specific goal or intention so it's important chunk your life down into contexts, chunk down again to resources that will serve you best in each context, and then chunk back up to the state you will need to be in in order to access those resources.

Again, you do not have to go in that exact order. You can start by identifying the state before you identify the resources.

What Are Some States You Do Not Want to Be In?

States of fear, anger, and panic are what I call scarcity states and they are extremely limited. Anger and fear can be useful to wake you up to danger or an injustice for example, but they are not good states to stay in.

We make bad decisions when we are fearful, angry, or panicked because these states create an extreme narrowing of our awareness. We need to narrow our awareness in order to focus but if the focus is too narrow you will cut yourself off from the resources you need to resolve the situation or perform at your best.

I would even say that panic is the state of no access to your resources, which is why you panic and it is why you always hear that you should never panic during a crisis. You probably, ideally, should never panic ever because it will not help you.

Every state has its limitations and in order to perform well we have to focus so it's better to map out ahead of time what resources and states are needed in every major context of your life so you can gather the resources you need and allow the resources you don't need to stay outside of your focus in order to achieve the outcome you want.

It is also important to be in a state that aligns with the proper context. When we're not aware of what states we perform optimally in for a given context we end up entering a professional context while still in a parenting state or we come home after work still in a professional state when it's actually time to be in a husband or wife state.

Greater awareness of your states will give you greater control over aligning your state with the right context so you're at your best in every area of your life. It will also give you more flexibility in managing and changing states to succeed in whatever context you are in.

Performance

You juggle multiple tasks at one time not getting anything done. You lose focus easily and gets overwhelmed with so many things to do. Distractions seem to be everywhere that makes it nearly impossible to accomplish anything.

Before you know it, your twenty-four hours in a day are over and you still have not finished the task you are supposed to do.

Time is an especially important resource. Once it slips out of your hands, there is no way you can turn it back.

We are all given the same number of hours. Many would say the difference lies on how we use those hours, but I would argue that attention is far more important than the time we have.

We can have all the time in the world, but if our attention is diffused everywhere, we will hardly get the results we desire.

As Tony Robbins has said, "Where focus goes, energy flows."

How the Brain Processes Attention?

The brain is a powerful organ that is capable of processing loads of information. It controls your behavior depending on how you shape it. It has magnificent qualities that is capable of rewiring neural connections to strengthen new habits and weaken poor behaviors.

However, it has a fundamental vulnerability that can affect your performance and productivity. The brain is overly sensitive to interference or being distracted.

The brain has limited cognitive control abilities which can affect your goals and your ability to fight distractions.

In the book The Distracted Mind: Ancient Brains in a High-Tech World, authors Adam Gazzaley and Larry Rosen presented a thorough explanation of how performance diminishes because of the interferences that the brain encounters.

Often, you have a specific goal in mind, yet something hinders you from successfully completing that goal. Interference is something that obstructs another process. It can be internally induced or externally inspired by sensory stimuli.

Interference can be in a form of distraction or interruption.

When you are bothered by the random thoughts in your mind, you are being distracted internally. When a notification from your phone or chatter around you steal your attention, you are being distracted externally.

Most of the time, you wish to ignore these distractions to accomplish your goal. You either win against them or they win against you.

Interruptions, however, happen when you make a conscious decision to engage in more than one task at one time. You are attempting to fulfil different tasks with different goals at the same time. This is what many calls as multitasking, but its nature is simply "task switching."

Many people are wired to believe that they are great at multitasking. They are very proud of it so much that they flaunt it on their resumés. Many employers also put heavy demands on their employees by requiring them to accomplish many tasks at the same time.

But the brain does not favor this kind of conditions.

Neuroscientist Richard Davidson found that key circuitry in the prefrontal cortex gets into a synchronized state during sharp focus.

The stronger the focus, the stronger the neural lock in which makes it easier to attend to a task.

During sharp focus, the brain maps the information you already know to connect it with what you are trying to learn.

Daniel Goleman shared in his book Focus: The Hidden Driver of Excellence:

"The optimal brain state for getting work done well is marked by greater neural harmony—a rich, well-timed interconnection among diverse brain areas. In this state, ideally, the circuits needed for the task at hand are highly active while those irrelevant are quiescent, with the brain precisely attuned to the demands of the moment. When our brains are in the zone we are more likely to perform at our personal best whatever our pursuit."

Attention is an especially important skill to master. It is difficult to do anything if you rarely have focused attention long enough to code it into your brain.

Attention is your key to open the door of productivity and better performance.

If attention is especially important for the optimal performance of the brain, why do we engage in interference-inducing behaviours?

Chapter Eight

You are your own Competition

We all start somewhere. We all walk into a new gym for the first time, sign up and contemplate what future goals we hope to accomplish there. We start out well, just trying to focus on ourselves and our own workouts, but sometimes we get lost along the way. We see other people in the gym lifting a certain amount of weight or executing a movement perfectly that we are too afraid to even try. As soon as we start comparing ourselves to other people and how we are stacking up- we are already losing ground on what we can accomplish. Our world loves to compare and compete and measure success based on the accomplishments of others.

We compare the clothes we wear, the neighborhood we live in, the car we drive, even the handbag we carry. We compare our job titles, our salary, our savings account, even our retirement age.

Unfortunately, these comparisons rarely bring any joy into our lives.

Instead, they make us miserable.

One reason is because comparisons by their very nature are unfair. We know ourselves better than we know others. As a result, we compare the worst we know of ourselves to the best we assume in others.

But there is another reason these comparisons result in lower life satisfaction: the trinkets we are competing for do not bring fulfilment. Job titles, square footage, and brand names on handbags are not the things that matter in life.

Your Only Competition is Yourself

Every time that you step into the gym or head out to do your workout you are getting fitter. You are getting stronger and you are one more step closer to accomplishing your goals. No one else can do that workout for you. No one can go on a run for you, they cannot lift that weight for you and unfortunately, they cannot do your burpees for you. You must do that work yourself to get to where you want to be, so

Why do we compare our work to other people?

Why do we get wrapped up in what other people are doing, or accomplishing?

We create our own journey, and we can expect results based on the work that we put in. Everyone is different and will progress at a different rate. The hard work that you are doing in the gym is amazing and you should be proud of the work that you have accomplished. No matter how small they may seem today, they will add up.

If you look on Instagram, Facebook and any other social media sites, the posts that you are seeing are almost all day to day success stories. What you hardly see are the posts coming from the days of pure grunt work – the fails, the misses, and the hard days that every single person has. Anyone you talk to that has been successful will tell you that it was not an easy road to get there. Anybody who you think is, "where you want to be," will tell you the hard work that is required. No one achieves their goals by sitting around and hoping they happen- or watching other people. Every person you see as successful will also tell you that they started anxious, afraid, and had many days along the way that they felt like they were not where they wanted to be.

You do not need to compare yourself to anyone except for the person that you were last year- last month- yesterday. You are so much greater and stronger that that person. You have come so far and achieved so much already. Allow yourself to continue to grow. Anything is possible- all you must do is believe in what you can do.

Today's you is better than the yesterday you. Tomorrow's you will be better than today's you. Do you and only you.

"My 10 Minutes" You Are Your Competition

Pen down situations when you do fall short and start comparing yourself to others.

At that moment, think what is it that caused you to do so?

How did it make you feel?

Did you like that?

If not, why not?

Then what are you going to do about it?

Focus on Results – Work Smart, Not Hard

In this book, I have occasionally challenged the notion that working hard is always a good thing. Sometimes, working hard means wasting your life on chores or wasting your life working for a company that does not value you.

Much better than working hard then, is to work smart. That means that you stop focusing on working for the sake of working and start working to get results.

This is where it becomes important once again to assess your past mistakes and look at what has worked and what has not. This will allow you to invest your time only where it counts and only where it matters.

Freeing Up Mental Space

And sometimes, this means finding ways to remove the unwanted distractions and clutter from your life. Work that does not take you closer to your goal is not work that is worth your time. Work that takes you away from the things you are passionate about is not worth your time.

And so, if you are currently spending half your evening washing up and cleaning the house... it's time to stop! You worked incredibly hard in order to earn money for your family – you traded your time for resources – and now the little time you have left you're going to spend washing up??

This is another cognitive shift you need to make to be truly successful – you need to start valuing your time more and be willing to spend your money to protect it. You need to recognize that Time > Money.

So instead of spending your time cleaning the house, why not hire a cleaner to do it? You've worked hard enough to deserve one and this way you can work on more fulfilling side projects (and earn back the money you're spending several times over), you can spend time with your family and friends, or you can spend more time enjoying the hobbies that you are truly passionate about.

Likewise, you can give yourself more time by investing in a dishwasher, a robotic vacuum cleaner or maybe even a service that will deliver you readymade meals to your door for lunch and dinner!

"My 10 Minutes" Free Your Mental Space

Make notes of what is distracting you constantly it seems to appear in front of you.

Distractive work, that takes you away from your passion. Make a list of them.

Sit and ask yourself how is that work going to help you achieve your Definite Major Purpose in Life?

Are you prepared to continue to contribute towards that work or are you going to say once, and for all STOP IT. Enough is enough? I want to dump them.

Now hereafter you would need to look at every time those distractions appear identify the opportunity loss if you continued to do that measly work instead of focusing your purpose drive tasks. Bring that opportunity loss every time you get distracted.

Invest in You

Do not think that this means you should not be spending time on your appearance though – you absolutely should. This takes us right back to our 'law of attraction' principle from the start of this book. To get the best jobs and to have the most success with the opposite sex, you need to look the part.

And to look the part, you need to spend time or money. You do not have the time to spend hours ironing and run a second business from home – so spend the money on your appearance, your step up in skill set, your continuous further education, books, seminars etc. Believe that this money is well spent. Have faith like your parents did, when they put money in your education some 20 years ago. Realizing that you will reap from that investment. They had the wisdom. What are you doing? Following your parent's footsteps? If not, why not?

That is how those incredibly polished people who just seem to excel in everything they do got that way.

Creating Business Models That Succeed

This 'results focused attitude' is also how you are going to design your business models and choose your projects. Think about the resources you already have available to you, the contacts you already know and the skills that you already possess.

If you are the editor of a magazine on a certain topic for example, then you have a huge captive audience. What business could you launch that you could aim at that audience?

And as I have said already before do not think about success in terms of what others perceive as success. A lot of people will try and start businesses that they think will 'change the world' or 'offer something completely unique'. But you know what? This type of business makes it much harder to find investors and much harder to market. If you want to make money quickly, if that is your goal, then you're often much better off just using a tried and tested business model that countless people have used before.

Do not invest huge amounts of money into a business before you have 'verified it'. Use the 'fail fast principle' by creating an MVP and seeing if it is successful before spending lots of time on it. This will also let you stay lean and jump between multiple business models.

If you're willing to look for the shortcuts and if you understand the most important variables in each equation, then you can often sidestep the work and jump straight to the good part – earning lots of cash!

Success really does not have to be as hard as everyone makes it out to be... You just need to the right attitude and some gumption.

Do not be Afraid to Switch Course

Once you've put everything we've discussed here into action and you've found yourself a dream to follow and a set of steps to get there, you will hopefully have some time to stop and smell the roses. What is the view like from the top? Is it everything you hoped?

How to Change Trajectory

Once again, many of us have some strange notions when it comes to what the 'right thing' to do here is. Because if they do not find it really is everything, they hoped... often they will be too prideful to admit it and will stay committed to that new way of life anyway! In this scenario, you are literally trapping yourself out of nothing but pride.

Do not be afraid then to admit your mistakes – and self-honesty is something that has come up a lot in this book. Admit your mistakes, address them as we have been doing elsewhere in this book and then decide how you will move forward without repeating those same errors. What is it you are not happy with? How are you going to make sure that you are happy next time?

Springboard to Success in Multiple Areas

Another thing to consider is just how you can take one success and turn it into the catalyst for far bigger and more far reaching successes.

Mark Zuckerberg, creator of Facebook, has been a rather successful online entrepreneur it is fair to say. However, while he has been incredibly successful, no one is perfect and there are perhaps ways in which he could be more successful still or more ambitious. Facebook was a huge hit, and it genuinely changes the way we interact with our friends and family. However other than various updates to Facebook (not all well received) it seems that Zuckerberg has had little else to unleash upon us since.

This is a shame when you consider the uniquely powerful position that Zuckerberg is in with Facebook. With millions of people all using his website he has one of the most powerful marketing platforms in the world at his disposal. If he were to unveil a new website, or a piece of software or perhaps something entirely different, then he could announce it through Facebook and if he did it right – he could have a guaranteed hit on his hands. Even if only 5% of Facebook's population bothered to click the link that would be a huge start by anyone else's standards. To be fair, he is starting to become a little more ambitious when it comes to his investment in VR etc.

Sidestepping for a moment let us look at the rather different career of Sylvester Stallone. He wanted to be an actor and was turned down from countless screen roles, before he eventually wrote the outstanding screenplay for Rocky. This was such a big hit with producers that they offered him millions to take it off his hands – but Stallone would not back down. All he wanted was to play the lead role. In some ways, Zuckerberg could stand to be a little bit more like Stallone. The point is – that once you have had success in one area, you then suddenly can chase almost any dream that you want to go after. Once you have changed one industry, one institution, then you can go on to bring about paradigm shifts in many others too. And this is particularly true on the web.

So if you currently have a huge website and you are making lots of money from Google AdSense – if that is the goal you set out with and that is what you achieved - don't stop there or you will be the victim of a lack of vision.

If you have a big audience, then you can really do anything you want to. For instance, you could open a shop on there, and you could very easily use the funds to make this into a real store if that should be your dream.

Always wanted to be famous. Then how about you introduce YouTube videos to your website where you know countless viewers will see them and subscribe?

Want to build the next Facebook? Well now you have a background in SEO and website design you can hire the programmers and get to it.

Got another side project? Well a link from your own sites with high PR will give your new seedlings the boost they need to get going. And likewise, it works the other way too – and if you have a successful Twitter page then you can use this to build up a successful site. In other words – pool your resources, be ambitious, and chase after your dreams. And once you've had one big success online, with your own business, or in some other arena... don't stop there – use it to fuel all of your others. That goes for you too Mark...

"My 10 Minutes" Springboard to Success in Multiple Areas

Jot down three key points you got from this segment that will enrich you in what you are currently doing. How could you value add to your current situation.

Step Back from Your Emotions

A lot of what we have discussed in this book involves being able to take a step back from your emotions and being able to take control of your fears and your stress. This is something that can be incredibly challenging for many people, but it is a highly worthwhile cause and one that will help you to be much more successful. This is what will enable you to take the right action, rather than the one that is the most comfortable and it is what will allow you to stay cool and calm under pressure.

How to Take Back Control

Controlling emotions starts by recognizing what emotions are. Emotions are hormones and neurotransmitters that are normally released in response to certain activity in the brain, or to certain changes within your body. You are often stressed because your blood sugar is low for example!

In other cases, you might be stressed and experiencing the 'fight or flight' response – which is essentially the release of neurotransmitters like cortisol an adrenaline.

By first recognizing that this is what your emotions are, you can immediately detach yourself from them to an extent. They are transient and they will pass – so do not pay too much head to those scared thoughts or those destructive unhappy ones. Wait until you are calm and happy before making any big decisions!

Another tip is to consider fixing your biology to fix your emotions. That might mean eating to remove the low blood sugar, or it might mean taking control of your breathing to regain that composure and to restore homeostasis in your body and mind.

Do not let your emotions take control of you – because they are just as capable of trapping you in a life you do not want as your circumstances are.

Once again, it all comes down to choose. You can choose to let your emotions control you, or you can once again recognize that this is a choice and refuse to let it happen. You get to choose how you respond to decisions, just as you get to choose what matters to you, what success means to you and how you are going to get there.

It's time to stop coasting by on the expectations of others. It's time to stop letting others dictate to you how you should live your life. As Jackie Chan once said: 'do not let circumstances control you, control your circumstances'.

And do not be afraid to dream a little bigger, a little outside the box and to take risks to make that happen.

It might not work out as you planned but at least you tried – and you have not failed until you stop trying.

Chapter Nine

ARCO Motto

Prior to leaving the work force as an employee, I had spent 15 years working for an Oil & Gas company, called ARCO starting off as an accountant culminating my work career as VP for Admin, Finance & Accounting, HR and IT. During that time, the wealth of information, experience acquired whilst going through the various roles of climbing up the corporate ladder and having a buffet of managers, leaders as role models to follow was immeasurable. At that stage I had not realized what I was internalizing and accumulating in knowledge, experience, cross pollination (interacted with people as far North as Alaska, and as far south as Falkland's) This exposure with people from different cultures, backgrounds and religions was the highlight of my stay with that company, where I learnt the most on real life education. This is what I am sharing with my programs. I learnt that true learning and development is not on the mainstream education, instead it was from the 3 E's - Mainstream Education, Experience, and Exposure. In time, as I journeyed through recognizing when I was working and helping a variety of people to step up in their life, I learnt the power of the acronym ARCO.

Now you must be wondering, "What is ARCO Motto". It is one of the things that I honestly believe in and has helped me grow. The main reason for me to share it with you is for you to understand who you can achieve success and growth in your life using a simple ARCO Motto:

1. Accountability
2. Responsibility
3. Commitment
4. Ownership

Accountability

There is a simple principle I follow:

Do not let your present and past circumstances define who you are and what you do moving forward.

In other words, don't place the hope of pending success in the hands of luck or chance. You create your luck with the decisions you make and the actions you take. Relying on someone or something to save you only handicaps the true power you have of thinking clearly, being creative and reacting quickly. Instead, charge your momentum through action, and good, positive, game changing things will begin to happen.

How to Be Accountable for You! – The Seven Step Process

So whether you're looking to make some major changes in your life or you just want to tweak areas a little, I can help you unleash your power and potential in order for you to turn your actions into the results you want in life. Let me tell you how you can do so...

1. *Be accountable for yourself.*

   Are you holding yourself accountable for the actions and inactions in your life? Answer this question honestly because no one is judging your position in life except you and you know where you want to be. Staying true to yourself and your goals should not be a chore, but rather look at it as a never ending gift to yourself, a strong mindset that when set into place will ensure you are taking the proper actions towards success, even if you are kicking and screaming along the way.

2. *Think as if your life depended on it.*

   "If it has to be, it's up to me"...this is a personal quote that I create for myself and use as a mantra in order to shift my mindset into a determined, creative mindset that doesn't allow for excuses to rest and allow complacency to set in. When you shift into a determined mindset, you will discover solutions and resources for perceived challenges that you may have believed were out of your control. If your life depended upon it, would you come up with an idea, solution, or strategy to save yourself? No doubt!

3. *When you cannot control your circumstances, do not let your circumstances control you.*

   Things happen in everyone life that doesn't go the way they plan, that doesn't mean you scrap the whole idea or goal, that means you need to focus on what worked, what didn't work scrap it, and find another way. It's called experience by the way and NOT failure and looking for sympathy for one attempt isn't going to do you any good. Thomas Edison attempted over 1000 times to get that one opportunity to make it right and it changed the world! Let your goal or idea do the same through the energy, focus and action you put behind it. Remember, whether you are encouraged by this article or someone else, the point is, get out there and do SOMETHING.

4. *You must want it MORE than you do not want it.*

I was playing basketball with my friend in the park one day and it was very windy and as I was coming up to the court he yelled out, "Ron! The difference in who wins today depends on who wants it the most." Not having our usual long-range jump shots in the arsenal made us both rely on creative ways to make baskets. Your goals are the same. Everything you set out to achieve will exact a certain price from you – energy, effort, patience, persistence. It's perfectly natural to want good things in life without paying the price but success comes when you hit that tipping point and began wanting your goal more than you dread the road to reaching it.

5. *STRETCH outside of the normal and breakthrough.*

Most times we follow the paths that were before us and that is fine, to get you started. But for you to follow your passion you must blaze your own trail, and that may mean trying something new and different even if it's uncomfortable and it scares you. Jim Carrey is a perfect example. Watching his interview with Oprah, he stated that he would drive his beat-up Toyota to Hollywood Hills and while overlooking Los Angeles visualize himself being this big actor and really internalizing the feeling. Then he pulled out his check book and wrote himself a check for $10 million dollars. In that moment two things happened! First, he drew a line in the sand with his personal resolve and secondly, he let go of the normal and tried something outside of his routine that he said and I quote "What will this hurt?" When you discover your own internal power, you will see that you have the right, the ability, to live your best life and create your own reality, and it's up to you to breakthrough even if what you have to do in faith scares you.

6. *Ask Yourself, Am I all in?*

We care more for things that we are committed to do, as oppose to doing just enough to get by. My mentor Jim Shead used to give our seminar team this empowering mini speech before we would meet people. He wanted us to be all into the people we were helping with no distractions. He would say, "How can you be all in when you're distracted by other things going on in your life? Leave your life outside those doors. If you are with me you are vested in me as much as I am vested in you and I need for you to be all in. Own what you are doing in that moment with that person." When you own something — no matter what it is, you make an investment that involves sacrifice. If you are not all in, you can walk away from anything without losing something. If you are really committed to achieving any goal you set out to accomplish, go all in.

7. *Make it happen! Make it so! Engage!*

I am a stone-cold Star Trek fanatic! I love Captain Picard's voice and especially loved when he would ask Data to set a course to an unknown galaxy and he would look out over the deck into space and say, "Let's see what out there....ENGAGE!" How do you do that? How do you make it happen? It starts by taking the first step...nothing more. You have the choice to fulfil your dreams or wallow in self-pity, playing the victim game. The choice is yours but understand that true success and accomplishment doesn't come with you achieving the goal, that's just part of the process. It is the process that the journey to accomplishment transforms you into a better person. And guess what? Once you know that it is possible, the only limitations you will have are the ones you create yourself. So......go see what out there for you to accomplishment... Make it so! ENGAGE!

So, if you are struggling with holding yourself accountable, know that you are not alone. I am right here with you, struggling to keep myself accountable as well – we're in this together. And it is not something that you will succeed the first time. You will make mistakes, but the key is do not be so hard on yourself and keep moving forward. We will get through it. And this 'getting through' will make us stronger. It is not easy now, and it may take us awhile, but it will be well worth it in the end.

Your Turn…Exercise Your Everyday Power

What are some of the things that keep you stuck or helps you get unstuck from pursuing your goals? Which one of these steps if applied in your life would help you move closer achieving your goals?

"My 10 Minutes" On Seven Steps

Working with the above seven steps, how could you be more accountable in the ways you do your daily activities List down three senecio where you will implement these seven steps. How would you do it?

Being Responsible

> **Do not go around saying the world owes you a living.**
> **The world owes you nothing. It was here first.**
>
> **- Mark Twain.**

Remember when you were growing up all you could think about was when you were grown up. We thought about the freedom and privilege we would have when we became adults. We kept saying, "Treat me like an adult", "Let me make my own decisions", and "Can't I come and go as I please?" Right? So here we are all grown up with the liberty and privilege only to find out it came with a heap of responsibilities. So now we are being held accountable for our behaviors and decisions.

"It is not enough to take steps that may someday lead to a goal; each step must be itself a goal and a step likewise." Johann Wolfgang von Goethe We are answerable for all our actions, our thoughts and our behaviors, whether deliberate or unintended. We make mistakes, and when they do, we need to take the situation into control and fix it.

There is an expression that says, "You are where you are because of who you are". Everything that happens in your life happens because of you, because of your behavior, words and activities.

How do you become a responsible person?

- Be accountable. If your children are lively, your partner bad-tempered, your co-worker intolerable, you are always responsible for how you react. You are completely 100% responsible for your communication and behavior.
- Stop blaming. Remember when you point your finger at others, three other fingers are pointing towards you. As you point that finger, the other person only becomes defensive, and the conversation takes a turn for the worst. Just because the other person is being foolish; does not mean you should act that way as well.
- Recognize what occurred. When you admit, "Yes, I did not call when I said I would," you remove the necessity to make up petty explanations. "I screwed up" is a three-word sentence, when followed up with "What can I do to make it better?" it makes people eager to forgive. Your integrity gets respect.
- Emphasize the positive. Keep a positive attitude as you go through each day. Have you ever noticed that people who do not take responsibility for their behavior are cynical and pessimistic? Anything that does not go right is always that other person's doing. They are eternal targets. When you assume responsibility for having the life you want, you shift your focus from what went wrong to what is right. As light shift in focus turns a loser into a champion.
- See yourself unmistakably. Taking responsibility means admitting both your weaknesses and strengths. It means accepting all that is great about you. Be kind to yourself. A responsible person does not discharge their achievements. You know you have noble and positive talents. Have a complete picture of who are. A responsible person continues to develop emotionally.
- Say "thank you." Receive the compliment When someone recognizes you, say, "Thank you." When someone is caring or gives you a gift, say, "Thank you."
- Practice healthy self-focus. Pondering too much about our problems, stressing endlessly about the tomorrows, regretting the past, and feeling sorry for ourselves can only lead to indulgent self- pity. It is draining. However, taking time to know what makes you tick, in a gentle, insightful way is the start of self-love and individual accountability.

"My 10 Minutes" Being Responsible

On a scale off one to ten self- assess yourself on each of the seven points above. One being least productive and ten being most productive. At the end of the exercise work, select three of the least assessed point and work on improving them by one point through the next 30 days.

We do not like to fail or worse yet to seem like we are failing. So, we set goals for ourselves and at the same time create a "fall-back card", we can play when we are not successful so that that we can blame someone or something. The more individual responsibility we take, the more control, and the more control we have, the more likely we will obtain our goal since there will be no reasons to use our fallback card if we fail.

Therefore, taking responsibility for our actions equals success. It also makes us feel good about ourselves and frees us of negative behaviour such as anger, fear, bitterness, resentment and uncertainty.

The Art of Commitment – Five Step Process

**One person with Commitment is worth more
than 100 people who have only an interest.**

- Mary Crowley

Achieving even the simplest of goals requires us to learn the meaning of commitment. Throughout our life, we are reminded of commitment, whether it's related to personal or business goals, and we realize that without committing, we can't achieve anything.

When you think about it, everything you ever achieved sprouted from a commitment you made; whether it's your children, your degree, your job, or even your house. Learning how to commit is not simply about making commitments, however, it is about keeping those commitments in the face of foreseen and unforeseen hurdles.

Here are a few of my favorite tips that will help you to "Commit" & Change Your Life:

1. Do not be involved, commit!

   Doing things half-hearted is the mother of everything that can go wrong.

"The difference between 'involvement' and 'commitment' is like an eggs-and-ham breakfast: the chicken was 'involved' – the pig was 'committed'."

When you want your project to succeed, you invest yourself in it fully. Why? Because you cannot afford to only be involved; being involved means you're not committed enough, and if you're not committed enough, that thing you've been working on, won't see the light of day. Do not chicken out.

You cannot work on several things at the same time and expect excellent results. Make sure you are doing one thing, and you are investing all you've got.

2. If you will not learn how to commit, someone else will!

There is someone out there who knows everything you know and they're probably not alone.

"Competing in sports has taught me that if I'm not willing to give 120 percent, somebody else will. "Ronald Mark Blomberg (Boomer)

We live in a highly competitive environment and truth be told, it's exhausting. So what are you going to do? Are you going to quit? Probably not, but why? You're wired to keep on fighting—every time you think you've reached rock bottom; you connect to an inner mechanism based on millions of years of evolution whose sole purpose is keeping us alive. It can be either by running and hiding so you'll be able to fight another day, or by making you fight tooth and nail to get what you need.

You probably heard about this fight-or-flight instinct.

In fight-or-flight mode, your pupils dilate, your heart rate goes up, and blood pressure increases with the purpose of getting more oxygen into your brain and muscles. This response allows you to give much more in a competitive environment... but guess what? the same happens inside the other guy's body. That is why the one who's more committed will be the last one standing.

3. Never give up, never give in!

Quitting is also a lesson; an expensive lesson if you ask me. You pay for that lesson with the time you lost, the energies you invested, and a major blow to your ego. However, sometimes you find yourself with your back to the wall and you need to take drastic measures to save the day.

Sun Tzu (the ancient Chinese author of The Art of War called it "desperate ground":

Throw your soldiers into positions from whence
there is no escape, and they will prefer death to flight.
If they will face death, there is nothing they may not achieve.
Officers and men alike will put forth their uttermost strength.

- Sun Tzu

Do you know why people quit? There are 3 major reasons:

- Perfectionism.
- Lack of faith.
- General inability to keep commitments due to a history of failures.

All three are bound to each other. The more you fail, the less committed you become. If you are less committed, you have less faith. If you do not have faith in what you are doing, every non-perfect condition can break your resolution. It is that simple.

Fight Perfectionism, fight lack of faith (whether in you or in others) and fight history to stop it from repeating itself!

Never give in! Never give in! Never, never, never.
Never—in anything great or small, large, or petty—never give in except
to convictions of honor and good sense.

- Sir Winston Churchill

1. Free your mind, and the rest will follow!

   Once you are committed to something, your mind becomes like a homing beacon. There are no more choices to be made, just a focus on the target in front of your eyes—smooth sailing.

The resolved mind hath no cares.

- George Herbert

But what happens when you suddenly change your mind? When the choice you have made is no longer as attractive as you previously imagined it would be?

2. Commit to something bigger than yourself

If you have problems committing, it will be beneficial to commit in a group setting. The most likely way to overcome the fear of commitment is to commit to something bigger than just you, and in a group, you will be to draw upon others for both motivation and support.

> **Individual commitment to a group effort—**
> **that is what makes a team work,**
> **a company work, a society work, a civilization work.**
>
> **- Vince Lombardi**

In a committed group, everyone works for the benefit of that group. A perfect example is trying to teach a child to swim on his own vs. with a group of kids his own age.

In conclusion, commitment allows us to fulfil our most basic needs and achieve our most sought-after dreams. It gives us purpose. It is never too late to learn how to commit.

"My 10 Minutes" The Art of Commitment

On a scale off one to ten self- assess yourself on each of the seven points above. One being least productive and ten being most productive. At the end of the exercise work, select three of the least assessed point and work on improving them by one point through the next 30 days.

Taking Ownership, The 12-Step Process

It all starts with taking back your life second by second, minute by minute. We begin by taking back ownership of our mornings and our evenings and then building out from there.

It is a simple concept but can be extremely hard to implement and stick with.

Like someone tackling Mt Everest, it begins with a small step in the right direction and then having the mental strength to continue step by step as you head towards the summit. We focus on that next step and not be overwhelmed by what lies ahead.

Here are 12 steps you can immediately put into practice to help take back and keep control over your life:

1. Create a morning ritual and take back control of the first 1-2 hours of your life.
2. Exercise for 15-30 minutes, this is as simple as a walk and observe the natural world around you.
3. Journal on 3 things you're grateful for and 3 things that will make today great every morning.
4. Take 5 minutes to reflect on the amazing life you have lived so far. Listen to music while thinking about this.
5. Take another 5 minutes to listen to a power song and tell yourself today is your day!
6. Call someone you love to let them know you appreciate them and why they are important to you.
7. Create an evening ritual and own your last 1 hour of the day.
8. Journal on 3 amazing things that happened today at the end of every day.
9. Plan tomorrow by chunking your calendar into hour blocks and add in what you're going to do in each of those hours.
10. Take 30 minutes to read or listen to something spiritual.
11. Kiss your kids, kiss your partner and let them know how much you love them from heart.
12. Let go of everything you need to do, it's now on your list, close your eyes and enjoy your sleep.

We are not trying to hit almost impossible home runs here. We are focusing on hitting our daily singles that add up over time. Developing new habits that allow us to slowly take back control and build a life by design.

And so, it all starts by being honest with the fact that perhaps our business owns us, and it is time to make a change.

Do yourself a favor, start tonight, take back your mornings and evenings. Start the journey of living the dream life that you deserve.

You might not have thought about it, but those same people you are helping now could end up being more successful than you and some areas and that could be a valuable relationship down the road. Most people are going to remember that you helped them for many years to come and not only would they be willing to do a favor if they are able to do so they might even seek you out and offer.

"My 10 Minutes" Taking Ownership

Identify the steps that you are currently not doing. Select at least three and work on incorporating them into your daily routine. Then move to the next three and so forth such that after four months all of these should be with under your belt.

Seek out Ways That You Can Help Others

Whether you are helping mentor other people trying to be successful in the same industry that you're in or you're helping your customers find exactly what they're looking for and making sure that you provide them with the best service possible, you're going to actually have to go out and seek ways to help people; they may not come to you. So, what are some of the ways that you can find people that you are able to help? How do you know that they need help? Most importantly, what do you have to offer that is valuable enough to teach others? This last question is important, not because there's something that qualifies you to be a great teacher above all other things, but because you're going to want to know the answer to that question so that you have the confidence to teach.

As for finding people to help, your customers will probably come to you but make it clear that if they're looking for something specific, even if you don't necessarily deal with it in your own store or business that they should ask you about it anyway because you might be able help. Make sure that you post this on your website somewhere and go to social media to offer help as well. As far as mentoring goes, there are forums all over the Internet with people that are seeking advice, some of them better than others. Try to find people who are actually serious about being successful, like-minded with your own values and goals and willing to accept your help. There is no sense in helping someone who isn't going to put in the work because this will not give you any of the benefits that comes from helping people.

Become Known as Someone Who Will Go Above and Beyond

You want your customers to be happy. This means good customer service but if you really want to shine, go above and beyond with every single customer that you get. Do absolutely everything you can do to solve the problem and make them happy and you will reap the rewards. They will talk about you to their friends, their colleagues, and their family members and when they need a product or service that you sell, they'll be back to buy from you again and again. This is how Amazon has become so successful, by cultivating a reputation for customer service that is matched by no one else.

Chapter Ten

Gratitude is Ultimate

There is nothing like achieving the success that you want to make you grateful, but eventually the newness wears off and you forget to be grateful. There are so many opportunities to be grateful each day and so many reasons to do so. For one thing, people around you will be happier and much more willing to spend time with you. You will also be happier yourself and will have a more positive attitude. You will also find that everyone will be more willing to help you when they know that you're grateful for everything that you have and everything that you receive.

People Who Feel Entitled

You have probably come across people who feel entitled. They somehow believe that they deserve to have success without working for it, even though all the other successful people in the world have had to work hard to get where they are. These people are always negative, they whine and complain about any work that they must do and believe that the world should be handed to them on a silver platter. If you are one of these people, stop! If you just know people like that, make sure you avoid ever falling into that trap because it is a pit of negativity that is difficult to crawl out of!

Be Grateful for Your Opportunities

Be thankful for the opportunities that you have. If you live in a developed country, think of all the people around the world who don't have the opportunities that you have. Think of people who not only don't have access to the Internet and the ability to start their own business online, but they don't even have access to clean water or electricity. The opportunity to build a business and achieve that much success is nothing to be scoffed at. If you have that opportunity, you are a very lucky person and you should be grateful for it.

Also, you should be grateful for the teachers that you have in the information that you are able to acquire, from the Internet or whatever sources you are using. You should be grateful for the teachers that you have, that they have the knowledge to teach and that they are willing to teach you. There actually are successful people out there who don't subscribe to this particular thought model, instead taking the approach that the more people they shared the secret of their success with, the more competition there will be, which will apparently somehow devalue their own success, even if it's not the same industry. However, most successful people are grateful for those who help them get where they are today.

You have probably heard of Tony Robbins. Tony is a motivational speaker, author, and highly successful individual. Even with as much success as he's had, and all the things that he has done to create this environment for himself, he is still immensely grateful to the people who helped him get where he is today. In a recent interview with success.com Robbins said that he is still grateful to his earliest mentor, a man named Jim Rohn, who motivated Tony Robbins when he was young. Follow Tony's example and be grateful because there are benefits; not only the ones mentioned in the first paragraph of this chapter, but also some amazing benefits for your business itself. Science can't seem to find a metric to measure, but people that are grateful for all the opportunities that they had and all of the people who have helped them, are more likely to be successful than those who are not, and are usually several times more successful.

Practice Being Grateful Until You Get It Perfect

It is okay if you do not feel that you're at the point where you can be very grateful. Like anything else, being grateful takes practice. You might actually have to think hard about what you have to be grateful for when it comes to your online business, or you may have to wait until you actually do have something to be grateful for. The point is, start changing the way that you think. This grateful attitude goes along with everything else in this book. You are just being grateful because you should, you are being grateful because it changes you as a person; it makes you a better person and it magnifies your success.

Start a Gratitude Journal

One of the things that you can do to become better at being grateful is to start a gratitude journal. A gratitude journal is when you sit down at the end of the day and write down some of the things that you are grateful for. You can use your computer; you can use a piece of paper and a pen or even a smart phone app if you prefer. Just if you spend a little time each day thinking about what you must be thankful for, writing it down and using it to further your success.

"My 10 Minutes" Start a Journal

As part of you Me time commence to put aside some time to practice daily journaling of your gratitude journal.

Ways That You Can Show Your Gratitude

One of the things that you can do to give back is use whatever assets that you have gained from being successful to help someone else. If you're an Amazon affiliate, and you're getting your first check from Amazon for just over $100, if you can afford it donated to charity, or take it down to your local soup kitchen to help buy groceries or even outsource some of the things that you need for your business so that other people can make money too.

If you can show the world that you are grateful, the world will keep giving you opportunities and information to help you be successful. It sounds fake, like some sort of new age philosophy, but it truly is the way this thing works and if you talk to anyone who has achieved a decent level of success they will tell you that positive attitude, gratefulness and a willingness to learn are all keys to success.

Conclusion

This book is intended to help the serious person desiring to achieve personal mastery to take the first steps towards their success. In this book, you learned how important mindset is when it comes to success. You have learned that it is the ultimate factor that stands between the average person desiring success and the person that achieves it.

You are able to take stock of yourself, learn what your current strengths are, and which ones you need to cultivate in the future as well as what weaknesses have kept you from success in the past. You can learn how to set yourself up with healthy mindsets instead and how to use that new mindset to take you as far as you want to go. Of course, this is no easy journey and it may take some time to develop that mindset. That is the reason, we had included throughout this book the *"My 10 Minute exercise"* wherever we though it to be important and emphasized incorporating that pattern for change into your daily practice. No one is expecting you to change overnight but hopefully, this book will help you take the first two steps towards success.

10 Action Steps to Take

Here is a step-by-step summary of all the things that you need to do to attain the success that you desire, based on the principles and information in this book.

1. Realize how important mindset is. Understand that your mindset is what will determine whether you're successful – for good or for bad. Know how to change your mindset so that you can steer it towards success.
2. Start your journey of Self-Discovery. Know what all your current strengths and weaknesses are. Know what skills you bring to the table, know which skills that you're going to need but that you

might need to hone and understand how to use the skills to achieve the success that you want.

3. Develop the Right Framework for success. You know that in the past, your mistakes have been responsible for you not achieving your goals. This time, tell yourself, it isn't going to happen because you control your mindset; it doesn't control you.

4. You are going to change your mindset to be healthy and geared toward success. No matter what your goals are from this time forward your mindset will be a positive one and that will change your life completely. Even if you decide never to open up your own business this will give you success in your marriage, your job and your interpersonal relationships.

5. You will know how to focus on the present and quit dwelling in the past.

6. You will know the proper way to set goals so that they are clear, concise and specific, and they give you the ability to create a roadmap to reaching them.

7. You know how to be the best self that you can be. You will understand the process of change and be actively working on it with the confidence of knowing that as of right now you truly are the best self you can be.

8. Understand how to value your time so that other people don't take it from you and so that you can use it to achieve the goals that will take you from here to wherever your success is. No one else is as important as you are when it comes to achieving your goals.

9. You will learn what the ARCO motto. You will start being more accountable for your actions, take responsibility of every situation in your life, start committing to your path of success and lastly, take ownership of your life.

10. You will be grateful for what you have currently, how to give thanks for each day and why this is great for your future success.

Now you understand what it really takes to manifest your Dreams.

Success Journey

Dream

Strategy

Goal

Action

Results

Let me emphasize one more time: For the above Success Journey Steps and the many other steps described throughout the book, it is not just working through the steps that will provide the end outcome. Yes, the mastery and working through the step is important, but not vital.

What is vital is working through the six inches between the two ears and an attitude shift from the neck up. It is this that will provide the paradigm shift required for Personal Excellence and it mastery such that it is ingrained in every cell of your being.

I hope this book has given you some food for thought and the drive to go out there and start making those changes!

Drive and Enthusiasm, gets you started.
Patterns of Excellence anchored and
rein-enforced is what keeps you going

- davidnair

Congratulations

You have taken the first step!!!!

Now Continue Your Journey to The Life You've have always wanted:

A life of significance

Let David Nair show you how......

Check out how David opens the platform and creates the awareness of what is available and how to tap into it for excellence and success, guiding through the phase of *Unconscious Incompetence to Conscious Competence*

By purchasing the book, attending the Webinar or Preview, you have demonstrated a profound commitment to enhancing the quality of your Personal, Business and Professional Life. David would sincerely urge you to look at taking the next step and registering for the Live Event. See where it will take you and where it took thousands of others in their journey of attaining a successful, fulfilled, and happy Life.

David Nair invites you to join him at his Online programs, Live Step-Up Workshops and Seminars to learn and experience more essential skills that can transform your life.!!!

In so doing You Create that LIFE OF SIGNIFICANCE and journey through it with contentment.

I-eXceL - Wired For Success   "Personal Excellence Blueprint"

A 4-week Online Session: Prerequisite to all sessions.

A 2-day Live Event

I-eXceL – Your Why   "Destiny – Choice or Chance"

A 4-week Online Session.

A 2-day Live Event.

I-eXceL - Coaching & Mentoring

(Three months of coaching for maximum clarity in all areas of your life.) Check David's linkedin profile, You Tube Channel playlist on Testimonials, and ask for personal reference checks on David's unique capability in coaching. You will never regret this transformation session…. A true step up in coaching.

The ultimate intent is to have a mastery and use the hidden power of your Body, Mind and Soul properly. How best to unleash the magic within each of you, such that you could reflect on your life to see the journey and be proud of the trail blazer of a life you have left behind.

A legacy "Your life of Significance".
Your Friend, Guide, Coach, Mentor and Role Model
- davidnair

For more information on any of the above Please communicate to: admin@davidnair.net

Why you should join David at these powerful Sessions?

David will steer you through the following key determinants in achieving the required transformation you deserve, to enjoy the life you have always wanted….

1. A greater understanding of your Purpose in Life.
2. Solution Driven and clearly know what you want out of Life
3. Effective Decision Maker

4. Action Driven person
5. Laser Beam Focused in all that you do eliminating distractions
6. Mindset of a Champion

Ladies & Gentleman take that step forward to make that decision. Do not hesitate, do not procrastinate. Make that decision now to step up...

Think where you were one year ago, three years ago. How much have you changed, how much have you grown? What would your life be like, if you stepped it up to overdrive gear? What would be the perspective if your saw your life from overdrive state.

Friends Take that step forward to make that Decision.

Always remember......

In Moments of Decision That your Destiny is shaped.

- Tony Robbins

Reach out and hold David's hand, walk alongside him, and paint your tapestry of Life. See how it unfolds and manifest your dreams and desires that you have always longed for.

Destiny becomes a matter of Choice, Not Chance.
You are the Master of your destiny.
Let's go play this game of life, the way it should be played.

- davidnair

Your Friend, Guide, Coach, Mentor and Role Model
- davidnair

Social Media Links

You are welcome
to follow and subscribe on any of
David Nair's
social media channels.

Facebook Profile: https://www.facebook.com/david.nair.98

Facebook Page: https://www.facebook.com/davidnaircoach/IXL

Facebook Page: https://www.facebook.com/davidnairixl/

Linkedin Profile::   https://www.linkedin.com/in/davidnaircoach/

Linkedin Page: https://www.linkedin.com/company/
davidnaircoach/

Websites: http://ixlincorporated.com/http://davidnair.net/

Blog: https://davidnairblog.wordpress.com/

Twitter: https://twitter.com/DavidNairIXL

You tube: https://www.youtube.com/c/DavidNair

Insta   https://www.instagram.com/davidnair_net/Email

Contact: support@davidnair.net

God Bless

Made in the USA
Las Vegas, NV
03 September 2021

29566117R00111